For Emily,
    An excellent im[...] good
friend. I hope you enjoy reading
the adventures with these gatekeepers as
much as I enjoyed writing them.

TAILS
of the
GATEKEEPERS

Elizabeth C. Chapman

Elizabeth C. Chapman

Xulon
PRESS

Tails of the Gatekeepers
by Elizabeth C. Chapman

Printed in the United States of America

ISBN 9781629525396

www.xulonpress.com

Dedication

This book is dedicated with love and appreciation in memory of all the dogs that have loved and protected their owners, handlers, and families, as well as their communities as K9 police dogs, and their nation as war dogs, and to honor the ones that still do. Their love, loyalty, devotion, and camaraderie have enriched our lives and continue to, beyond measure.

Table of Contents

Preface

One of the first things we did when my husband, Erick, and I started our lives together was get a dog. I'm not sure where my incredible love for dogs and the desire to have one came from as I was never allowed to have one growing up. Perhaps it was because I got to know my friends' dogs and saw that they just love you unconditionally, something I felt I desperately needed in my life. But getting our first dog was the beginning of some great adventures that have continued for more than forty years.

Our first dog was a Golden Retriever we named Rufus. While we loved him dearly, Rufus was an escape artist and we found ourselves unable to provide for him the type of permanent enclosure required to keep him home and safe. We spent a lot of time looking for Rufus as he explored the beautiful Northern California locales. Finally, out of love and caring concern for him, we found Rufus a safe home that already had a couple of retrievers and that could provide for Rufus all that he needed.

We learned a lot from Rufus! We learned what kind of commitment it takes to brush a long-haired dog so that people could sit on your furniture. While many people would love to have a fur coat, getting one shed from a

Golden Retriever is not generally what they have in mind. We also learned how to care for a dog that gets carsick, how to dog-proof our house so that things are not broken in the course of daily life, and mostly how to balance loving our dog without letting him take over.

Erick and I have long since figured out that we are dog people and likely will always be. We would not trade the extra measure of love and joy we've received from our dogs and the fun we've had and continue to have with them for anything. We consider each and every one of them a gift and wanted to share these gifts with you!

Acknowledgments

My thanks to my wonderful husband who has not only let me have all the dogs we've had over the last forty plus years but has enjoyed every minute with them. He has supported all my efforts in training them and showing the ones that were show quality, but mostly has shared my love for them as family members. I'm so thankful for him as my life partner.

My sincere thanks goes to the Santa Clara Police Department who has been most gracious in allowing me to tell the story of their K9 Unit. The K9 Unit, under the direction of Sergeant Kevin Fraser, blessed me with the opportunity to watch them train with their dogs; they patiently answered my questions, opened my eyes to all that they do for their community, and even set aside time so that I might take the pictures that add so much depth to the story. It's been a most memorable experience, one for which I'm grateful.

I'm also thankful to my daughter, Erin, my son, Michael, and my friends who have allowed me to share their favorite dog stories. Many thanks also to all the wonderful people I've met and gotten to know in the process of writing this book—not to mention their wonderful, hard-working, loving, and sometimes crazy and kooky dogs. All of the dogs in the stories that I share in this book I consider unique and of great value. These gracious people and their dogs have all made a difference in my life, and I thank God for allowing our paths to cross. My best wishes to all of them with my hopes of staying in touch.

I want to thank Mike McCartney so much for sharing his amazing talent in designing the caricatures that illustrate some stories that there are no pictures for. He has greatly enriched the quality of this book. (www.mccartneydogs.com)

Finally to my editor, Patti Lee, my unending thanks for all the encouragement, hard work, direction, and guidance to help me in my desire to make *Tails of the Gatekeepers* a work of excellence.

Introduction

Over the years I've developed a deep, heartfelt understanding as to why dogs have often been referred to as man's best friend. You get a good dog and you have a friend for life that is never too busy to spend time with you, will listen to your secrets and never repeat them, will lick away your tears when you're utterly distraught, cuddle up with you when you're lonely, and with great exuberance share your excitement when your joy is full.

This is NOT a book about guard dogs but about dogs that are loved, are family, and as such play a natural part in protecting us in matters of the heart. As I reflect on the many adventures my husband and I have had with our dogs, there were times of great joy, some frustrations, moments of embarrassment, times of tears and mourning, some hard work, but mostly comfort, a lot of fun, and much laughter!

The stories I'm sharing in this book are mostly from personal experience, but I've also asked some of my friends and other wonderful dog owners/handlers I've met to allow me to share a few of their most memorable dog experiences. Some of the stories are inspirational, some are sad, some are funny, but all are truthful reflections of people who have had some exceptional dogs that do amazing things. Many of the dogs in these stories are AKC registered, accomplished dogs. If you would like more information as to the meaning of the prefixes and suffixes adjacent to the dogs' names, go to: www.akc.org/events/titles.cfm

For those of you who love your dogs as part of your family, I hope these stories are a source of great entertainment as I'm sure you'll be able to relate to many of them. I also hope the stories will be a source of encouragement for you to know that you are not alone during those embarrassing and/or frustrating moments and you will find new ways to be able to keep those times in perspective. And I also understand the depths of the loss you feel when you lose that precious canine friend.

For those of you who don't have dogs, my hope is that you'll just sit back and enjoy the adventures with us. My goals are that many will learn about some lesser known breeds, that some breeds will be seen in a new light with new understanding, and that we will all find a new level of appreciation and respect for our canine gatekeepers.

Chapter 1

Benji and Justin

(Benji) Benjamin Von Der Lorelei UD
(Justin) Justin's Gypsy Lord CD

I am combining the stories of Benji and Justin together partially because we had them at the same time but also because their adventures were often intertwined, making it impossible to truly tell the story of one without the other.

It was a couple years after we had to find Rufus a new home before we got another dog. Actually we got two new dogs and a cat. We were living in a county park where my husband, Erick, was the resident ranger, and he also patrolled as a reserve deputy with the Humboldt County Sheriff's Department. He got a German Shepherd we named Benji, I got my first Doberman, Justin, and together we got our calico cat, Sammie.

You'd think I would have learned from Rufus that if you get a dog with a long tail, you should expect to have precious items swept off the coffee table when the dog goes by. I realized this too late because Benji was already family. Justin of course was short haired with a short tail, and I immediately sensed that Dobermans, with their other wonderful qualities as well, would become the dog breed for me.

Justin and Benji with Erick

Benji was later to become Erick's constant companion as Erick took care of his responsibilities at the park. Campers sometimes got rowdy and Benji and Justin both were wonderful deterrents to campground visitors getting out of control. Benji knew his basic obedience very well and Erick would often leave him on a "stay" command in the truck with the dome light on and the door open. Erick would then approach the unruly park guests and courteously remind them of the park rules, especially the "quiet after 10 pm rule." If the guests responded appropriately, Erick would get back in the truck and leave. However, if they were resistant to complying with park rules, Benji gave a convincing backup performance by instantly coming through the crowd to sit by Erick, alertly watching the guests with no more from Erick than a simple whisper or hand command.

Not once, in all the time we lived in the park, was Benji called upon to do more than demonstrate his basic obedience skills.

We built a six-foot, redwood fence around our mobile home partially to protect our home from uninvited company but also to ensure that Benji and Justin would safely remain within the borders of our premises. One night when we had already been at the park for some time and Benji and Justin were already adults, their wonderful presence took on a comedic turn. There was probably a half an acre within our fence, including the area to the front and left of the gate where Erick and I had stockpiled firewood that came up to probably four or five feet of the six-foot height of the fence.

This particular night Erick had gone on patrol with the deputy assigned to our area, but they were called to a more remote part of their jurisdiction. I found myself alone to handle some drunken guests who apparently decided that it might be fun to harass the resident ranger. They were throwing bottles against the gate and saying some things that weren't appropriate with the likely intent of getting a response from us. I wasn't about to have them believe no one was home so as calmly as I could I went to deal with the situation. Benji and Justin were both with me, and when I let the dogs out, of course they got to the gate first. As an adult, Benji was a great watchdog. I let our visitors know that a deputy sheriff was on his way, which ended the throwing of the bottles, but the taunting continued.

As Benji paced the inside of the gate and continued to bark, Justin, who was less vocal, climbed up on top of the stockpiled firewood and peered over the top of the fence.

Since this was at night and Justin was black, he went unnoticed until he started to bark. I had no idea that right then on the other side of the fence, one of the drunks decided to use the fence as a bathroom. With his trousers still down around his ankles, he looked up into Justin's bared teeth merely maybe four feet above him. I had never before seen anyone try to run with their clothing down around their ankles, but run he did. Of course that along with his scream alerted everyone else to the presence of a second dog and they quickly dispersed. The deputy arrived shortly thereafter ensuring the final departure of these particular guests. When I came out with our pooper scooper to clean up the mess and told the deputy why it was necessary, he assured me that next time, he would come faster so as not to miss all the fun. (The deputy hadn't wasted time coming, but he had the presence of mind to put a lighter twist on a scary situation for me. I thought that Police Humor 101 must have been an addendum to his Post Certificate. And I was thankful.)

When Erick and Benji were gone making rounds in the park, Justin remained with me. Since they were both going to be working dogs, I alternated taking Benji and Justin to obedience class. I quickly realized how much I enjoyed working with dogs, and Erick helped follow through by also working with them at home. The dogs learned quickly—at least Benji did. I don't know if I felt inspired or if it was a moment of craziness but I decided that I would show these dogs in obedience trials. Justin didn't like to show all that much but Benji did and he shone in the obedience ring.

Whether it is in Novice, Open, or Utility, every dog enters the competition ring with 200 points. Then as the dog goes through the exercises, points are deducted with each error. A few points are deducted if the dog makes minor errors such as not sitting straight or not remaining exactly in heel position. Big mistakes, like getting up on the long sit, automatically mean a non-qualifying score. The dog must earn a qualifying score in every exercise in three separate AKC trials to earn each title. Many times, Benji won his class and on occasion was even the highest scoring dog in the trial.

Benji "Highest Scoring Dog in Trial"

Before I had a chance to get a swelled head thinking I was such a great trainer, Benji taught me a lesson about humility and the importance of having a loving, forgiving attitude and definitely a sense of humor. When Benji was ready to compete for his Utility Title, I entered him in a number of shows not expecting that he would necessarily pass with every attempt. On this particular weekend we were entered in three shows, Friday in Eureka, Saturday in Santa Rosa, and Sunday in Petaluma. Benji had actually already finished his Utility Title but since we were already entered, we went to compete for the working experience. Friday was a great day. Benji took first place in the Open B class, first in the Utility class, and was highest scoring dog in the trial. I was so proud!

We arrived at the show on Saturday and Benji, with absolutely no forewarning, had a total meltdown. I have no idea why, but in the Open B class, the only thing we passed was the heeling. With his tail happily wagging no less, Benji walked through the broad jump, around the high jump, did not retrieve the dumbbell, did not drop on recall, lay down on the long sit, and got up on the long down. Let's see, have I forgotten anything?? I was grateful he didn't run out of the ring! (Not that he ever had, but I was so shocked that I didn't know what else to expect.) My judge, as diplomatically as he could, told me my dog was clearly not ready to show but encouraged me not to give up. I was so embarrassed, but all I could do was laugh.

Speaking of laughing, the judge in the next ring was a well-known obedience judge who I had actually shown under the previous day. He had already finished with his class and was watching Benji's performance with great amusement. I saw him laughing, but in faith I believe he was laughing with me, not at me. He came over to our ring, joined in my conversation with my judge, and casually mentioned to my judge that

Benji, in fact, was already a Utility Dog who happened to be the highest scoring dog in the previous day's trial. By then, we were all laughing. They both then encouraged me with the fact that no matter how experienced a handler you become or how well-trained your dog is, there will be days like this. After Benji's memorable performance that day, I made a note to myself to always be ready for anything and to get upset about nothing. Just love the dog, have fun, and enjoy the process.

You would think that these wonderful, protective, mature working dogs would not be prone to doing anything really stupid. While we lived in the park, there were times we had other animals. We raised rabbits, chickens, a goose, and we even had a goat that I milked twice a day. Our desire and plans for self-sufficiency included harvesting the fruits of our labor. So at one point, we decided to put rabbits in our freezer for food, and Erick was going to tan the rabbit skins to make slippers and vests for Christmas gifts.

The tanning process is very labor intensive and after spending days scraping, stretching, and soaking the skins in salt brine and other solutions to preserve and soften them, the final task is to soak and rinse them in soapy water before drying them for use. We were at the last stage of the process and had several buckets of soapy water with rabbit furs in them when we left to go to town and see a movie.

When we arrived home, we knew something wasn't right—kind of like when you come home and your kids are really quiet and immediately you wonder what exactly they have been up to. Whatever it is, it's not likely to be good. We saw Benji and Justin right away, but we weren't greeted with their usual enthusiasm. Erick was the one to notice that the buckets of soapy water were tipped over and empty. Though I was hard pressed to believe it, it wasn't rocket science to figure out what happened. That evening the dogs were especially thirsty and were hiccupping soap bubbles for the rest of the night. And for the next several days Benji and Justin were leaving little fur balls all over the yard as the rabbit skins passed through their digestive systems. Our cat Sammie just watched them with a smug look on her face and purred.

Erick and I spent two and a half wonderful years living in the park—working, playing, and enjoying our dogs and cat. We took a lot of nature hikes, which, believe it or not, Sammie often joined us on. One of us had to carry her if or when we had to cross the Van Duzen River, but otherwise she kept up on her own. I think she must have thought she was at least part Doberman because I often would find her sleeping with Justin in his house. When we moved to Concord in 1976, we all moved together, ready for the new adventures ahead.

Sadly, not long after our move, we lost Justin to a serious illness. Though we missed him very much, I was grateful to know that he wouldn't suffer any longer. About a year later, we felt ready to add a new member to our family.

Chapter 2

Rischa

Nilee's Tomatoe Paste CDX

Rischa was the first Doberman I ever chose based on pedigree alone. She joined our family a year after we moved to Concord and turned out to be everything I could have hoped for and more. Rischa was a red female, beautiful, incredibly smart, very protective, even more loving, all the things a great Doberman should be. From the first day she came to us, she was easy to work with and was so gentle with our baby, got along with Benji, and even made friends with Sammie. Rischa melted my heart. She came everywhere with me and was my best friend. I started training her at four months because she was clearly ready. She loved to work and caught on to everything quickly.

My son, Bryan, was an infant when Rischa arrived into our lives, and I think at some level she believed that Bryan was hers. By the time Bryan started walking, she was a young adult. One day I was out in front of our house talking to a neighbor on a lovely summer day with Bryan and Rischa playing under my ever-watchful supervision. At one point Bryan started toddling off toward the edge of our lawn and the sidewalk when I got up to go get him. Rischa got there first, latched on to the back of Bryan's diaper, and started gently pulling him back. Bryan started crying and my neighbor got upset thinking Rischa was hurting him. Bryan wasn't hurt; he just didn't appreciate Rischa correcting his boundaries. I picked Bryan up and brought him back to where my neighbor and I were sitting. We both looked at the back of Bryan's diaper and there was not so much as a mark on it.

From that moment, I knew that Rischa would be a wonderful mother's helper with my children. Not long after that, I found myself expecting my daughter, Erin. Rischa, sensing my delicate condition, so to speak, was more protective than usual. She was very attentive to my every need, and I was wondering, as smart as she was, if I could teach her the art of doing dishes or cleaning the floor after Bryan, but alas, when I asked her, she just looked at me as if to say, "I think Mom's losing it."

Rischa was a working dog extraordinaire. She loved to work and finished both her CD (Companion Dog) and CDX (Companion Dog Excellent) before the age of two with most of her scores at 195 and above. These are the first two levels of obedience titles awarded by the American Kennel Club, and she just came by this ability naturally and truly lived up to her pedigree. If she ran, she ran full out; if she jumped over the high jump, she'd clear the jump by a foot. This little girl knew how to fly, and she was incredible to watch. And her tail never seemed to stop wagging even though she was all business. One of the shows I had entered her in was outside on a freshly cut green lawn. When I called her on the recall exercise, she came and sat in front of me waiting for the next command. I was waiting for the judge to say, "Do your finish," but instead the judge came beside me and was looking down at Rischa. The judge finally did say, "Do your finish" and then commented that while Rischa was sitting absolutely still looking at me after her recall, there was a wonderful visible "swish" in the grass behind her as that cute little Doberman tail was wagging back and forth.

Rischa "Highest Scoring Dog in Trial"—Photo by Bennett Associates

One beautiful spring day, a friend of mine and I were working our dogs out at a local park, preparing for an upcoming show. We had set up our jumps and took turns going through our open exercises. One of us would call out the command while the other worked her dog. We were on one side of the field, and on the other side at a considerable distance were some ladies playing softball.

We had been there awhile and it was again my turn to work Rischa. I had just sent her over one of the jumps and she was returning to come and sit in front of me when I noticed sudden movement out of my peripheral vision. At the same instant that I turned and saw a woman with her hands in the air and a baseball mitt on her left hand running directly for me, Rischa saw her too and immediately went to my defense. I was startled but not as much as the woman was when Rischa bit her. The woman was only maybe five or six feet from me at the most when Rischa reacted. After the shock that Rischa had bitten someone, I asked the woman what she was doing and told her how sorry I was that I didn't see her until the last second! She said she was chasing a very long fly ball that had landed on the other side of us.

The woman actually took responsibility and told me that she should have known better. She saw us working our dogs from a distance and should never have come running directly toward me, especially with her hands up in what she could understand Rischa clearly interpreted as a direct threat. She came back to the house with us, and I showed her Rischa's shot records as she had asked. I offered to pay for the doctor if she felt the need to go but, to her credit, she said she would use this experience as a lesson to keep in mind to be aware of her surroundings. It was a reminder for me too to be more aware of what's going on around me, especially when I'm out working my dog. At the time, as sorry as I was that Rischa had bitten someone, I had the realization that for the first time in my life I had experienced what it felt like for me personally to be protected. And it was amazing.

Rischa with Handler Gene Haupt

Benji and Rischa took their responsibilities for protecting our home very seriously. One day after I had been out running errands and was coming home, I saw multiple police vehicles cruising our neighborhood. Other police units were stopped at strategic locations. Since I lived there, I stopped and asked one of the officers what was going on. He told me that they were looking for several young men who, after a time of being pursued by the police, had abandoned their vehicle and were fleeing on foot in this neighborhood. I thanked the officer for the warning about the situation and went home.

I hadn't been home too long when I heard Rischa barking and growling. Since Rischa seldom if ever barked without good cause, I immediately went out to see what the problem was. And, lo and behold, Rischa had cornered a young man against our back fence with Benji backing her up a few feet behind her. It didn't take but a moment for me to figure out that this was likely one of the people the police were searching for. As long as he didn't move (which he didn't), Rischa made no move towards him but held him at bay against the fence. The guy started yelling at me in the most colorful language to call my dogs off, but I had a better idea. I reminded him that he was the intruder in their yard. I also told him I would be right back (that didn't seem to make him feel any better) and left him there in Rischa's most capable care.

I hurried out front, flagged down one of the officers, and apprised him of the situation. He called for backup and then followed me into our yard. Needless to say, the young man hadn't moved a muscle in light of standing before Rischa's bared teeth. When the officer told me he could take over the situation, I called Rischa back and she came to my side. The moment I called her off, the guy jumped over the fence into the neighbor's yard probably thinking of freedom at last. However he jumped right into the presence of another police officer who was waiting for him. The officer thanked me but especially thanked Rischa and Benji for a job well done.

Bryan was not yet three and Erin was a young baby when we bred Rischa. When it was time for the puppies to come and she was in labor, I prepared a place for her in the master bedroom. I blocked off our room so that she wouldn't be bothered, but somehow Bryan managed to get in. I had momentarily gone into the kitchen to get something for her when I heard Rischa growling. I immediately went to the bedroom to see what was wrong and caught Bryan swinging his plastic flatbed truck at her. Rischa barked at him and scared him but never made a move to bite. It had not been long since I'd been in labor and remembered vividly how it felt. I marveled at the excellence of the character of this dog.

Due to unforeseeable circumstances, Rischa died at the age of three from a virus that prohibited the growth and functioning of her kidney. We left no stone unturned in an effort to save her, but it was determined at a state-of-the-art veterinary facility that her death was imminent and nothing could be done. I loved Rischa so much. Once it was determined that there was no hope, I loved her enough to not prolong her suffering, and I let her go.

After Rischa was gone, I thought that every dog-loving person should be lucky enough to have a dog like her at least once in their life. A dog that was so loving, incredibly easy to train, trustworthy in every situation, faithful to a fault, an exceptional gatekeeper. It's been thirty-five years ago now, and I still miss her and think of her when I see a dog tenderly watch over young children or fly like the wind over a jump.

Chapter 3

JT

Aldenhan's Counterstrike

JT was a lovely red male Doberman who joined our family in the fall of 2003. The first time I saw JT with his littermates, he reminded me of a regal lion who stood aloof and majestic. He carried as much of a commanding presence as I'd ever seen in a puppy. Unfortunately, he was not at all like that in reality. In fact, JT, if he had been human, would have been referred to as a practical joker, the class clown. He even looked like one to me. He came with his ears cropped, one of the longest crops I'd ever seen. I hoped he would eventually grow into those ears, which he did, but when he was a young puppy, I thought his ears were long enough to get HBO.

In addition, nothing in the house that wasn't nailed down was safe. He walked off with shoes, socks, various other items of clothing, pillows, kids' toys, dog toys, eating utensils, the list seemed endless. When he was caught with them, he would smile pretending such innocence. His lips would curl as if snarling but in fact he was smiling. People who didn't know him would interpret his smiles as aggression, but I would honestly say that he was just teasing. In fact, that's how he got his name. JT stands for "Just Teasing."

Most often when I think of JT, the first image I have of him is sitting in my husband's lap. Yep, JT was a seventy-five pound Doberman Pinscher who was definitely a lap dog. No one was truly exempt from this honor unless they made it clear to JT that his presence on their lap was not welcome. If you're thinking that having JT in your lap would indeed be a scary thought, in his defense I must say that he was usually very much a gentlemen about it. He would ascend to one's lap gently putting one paw up at a time and finish his ascent with great care and precision so as to not cause discomfort. The exception was the occasion when my daughter, Erin, or my son, Michael, would come over, both of whom JT loved dearly. JT, upon seeing them, would take a flying leap into one of their laps. I'm thankful to say that Erin and Michael's love for JT would override the momentary discomfort of a big dog flying into their arms.

JT was in some ways my problem child. It was hard keeping weight on him. Eating was not a priority, and we ended up going to great lengths to feed him healthy foods that he would actually eat. Most often, I had to stay with him. Once I left the room, JT would stop eating and follow me wherever I went. He definitely suffered from separation anxiety, so leaving him at a pooch hotel to go away for a few days was seldom possible. He was also a shredder. He destroyed his bedding, his toys, and even his woobie (a blanket that dogs suck on, much like the way a young child might use a pacifier or favorite blanket). There were times I thought I should have named him Conan, the destroyer. I got to know the people at Anjan's, our food supply store, very well as I was frequently replacing JT's bedding and toys.

One day one of the salesman showed me a new toy they got in, a Frisbee made out of Kevlar, yes, Kevlar, the material that police officers' bulletproof vests are made from. "Finally," I thought. Something that will last! A few days later, I meekly returned the Frisbee in multiple pieces to the store. One huge praise on JT's behalf was that once he got over his puppy antics, JT only destroyed his own things, not ours.

JT had some interesting quirks. He would often sit next to me or under the piano bench when I would sit down to play. Though he never had any classical training, he loved Mozart more than any other composer. Don't ask me how he knew which pieces were Mozart because I have no idea. But he somehow seemed to know. Sometimes he would sit with his head on my lap and just listen.

He also had a great appreciation for Christmas carols. The first Christmas he was with us he was four months old and I was preparing vocal music for the upcoming Christmas program. Here was a dog that was seldom still as a puppy unless he was asleep, but JT would sit in front of me staring at me while I sang. The music almost seemed to comfort him.

JT was, in fact, a very vocal dog. This was most evident when Erick and I would go somewhere and then return home. We may only have been gone less than an hour, but when we arrived home, we would kiddingly say that we prepared ourselves to be "told off." The minute we'd open the door, JT would be right there talking (loudly, I might add) as if to say, "Where have you been? How could you leave me here? You've been gone so long. I have missed you!" Then he'd forgive us as we gave him lots of love, but inevitably he'd have to have the last word.

JT was also an incredible dog in many ways. When he was a puppy, my daughter, Erin, and grandson, Josh, were living with us, and they had a calico cat named Cassie. Cassie was not happy with JT's arrival, but JT thought Cassie was wonderful. As he grew up, he annoyed Cassie, but he was always good to her and just wanted to play. In time, Erin and Josh moved out with Cassie, but we saw each other often and JT, much to Cassie's chagrin, always had an affinity for her.

A couple of years passed and Erin was living in a condominium when one day Cassie got out and disappeared. This was in early November that year, and we all spent time and energy looking for her, leaving no stone unturned in an effort to find her. At the end of December, we had pretty much given up on ever getting Cassie back, and Erin decided to take a six-month job working at Ketchikan General Hospital in Alaska. Erin kept the condo during her absence, and my husband and I looked after it. Periodically, as I went to check on her place, I continued to look for Cassie but to no avail. Erin returned at the end of July which was then eight months after Cassie's disappearance.

One day when I was going to visit Erin and Josh, Erin asked if I would bring JT because she had missed him so much. As we were visiting, JT made it clear that he needed to go outside. Erin offered to take him out and I stayed inside playing with Josh. All of a sudden I heard, "Mom! Your dog is out of control!" I ran out to help her and saw that JT was out at the end of the leash tugging and straining for all he was worth. I took his leash and found myself being dragged around buildings, trees, and bushes. I was carefully watching the ground and my footsteps so I wouldn't get hurt, and followed JT. Clearly something was up and this was a dog on a mission. He finally stopped in front of a fence, jumped up against it, and when I looked up, there was Cassie. She was very thin and raggedy looking but there was no mistaking that it was her. It was then we realized that even after all that time, JT had caught Cassie's scent and had been tracking her. Thanks to JT, Cassie was home. My daughter hugged JT's neck with tears flowing, and for some time after that she would bring JT yummy leftovers for a finicky dog's palate in gratitude for him finding Cassie. JT was a hero.

JT loved to hike, camp, and kayak with us. One of his favorite places was Sterling Lake up in the Sierras where we usually went every year. JT would go around our campsite and establish an invisible perimeter that he would faithfully guard. He would get especially annoyed when birds had the nerve to fly through our campsite's airspace. He took this very personally and would chase them away. One day he spent a good part of the morning chasing the same birds away, and the moment he turned his back the same birds would return. Neither the birds nor JT were willing to give up.

Our campsite was right at the shore, and my daughter Erin and I were sunbathing at the edge of the lake where there was a nice grassy area ending with a maybe two-foot drop-off. It seemed the birds had decided to taunt JT by flying back and forth about six feet or so off the shoreline. JT would run along the shore but clearly the birds were out of his reach. Finally, JT had had enough. He backed off the shoreline a good ten to fifteen feet, and the next time the birds flew by, JT ran all out straight for the birds. When he reached the shore, he seemed to literally fly through the air at the birds with all four feet extended. He looked magnificently menacing! The birds, clearly unprepared for JT's assault, squawked in dreaded fear and dispersed. It was at about this point that JT realized he was in midair over the lake, and much to his dismay, he discovered he couldn't walk on water. With a most sheepish look on his face, he fell straight down into the cold lake. Of course he was only a few feet off shore so he easily swam to shore and was perfectly fine, but the look on his face at the moment of truth was absolutely priceless. This was one lesson he never forgot!

Except for tracking, JT didn't enjoy working. He was well trained in the basics to the point that we could take him any-where safely, but he would never have a show career in obe-dience. The level of his obedience was put to the test in July of 2008. We have a whole-house alarm system that we had some functional issues with when we first installed it. One day I had gone to do some shopping when I got a call that the alarm had gone off and the police were on their way to my house. I immediately turned around and headed for home.

Arriving at my court, I saw six police cruisers stationed at various locations around the court. After showing my ID,

I was allowed to drive up to my house where a police officer stopped me, asked me again for my ID, and then proceeded to tell me that the police were responding to a panic button alert. I was immediately concerned that my husband, who had been working out back, might have fallen off the roof and needed emergency help. I wanted to go to him but the officer detained me right where I was standing in the driveway.

The police had already opened our front door and quickly determined that no one was inside the house. The officer then told me that two officers (with guns drawn, I might add) were approaching the rear of the house from either side to assess the situation. I was to wait; the police officers would handle the situation. As I stood there gathering my thoughts, I found myself staring at my wide open front door. Then it hit me! "My dog...where's my dog?? He knows not to leave the threshold of the house; he's perimeter trained, but where is he?" The officer looked back to me and said, "You mean the Doberman?" "Yes," I replied. "Oh," the officer said, "He's in the back of my squad car." The officer must have seen a bewildered look on my face because he reassured me saying, "He's not under arrest or anything. When I opened the front door, the dog greeted me. I saw that his collar and leash were hung up by the door, so I called him, put his collar and leash on, and told him to heel, which he promptly obeyed. I took him to the squad car to keep him out of harm's way."

I turned to look at the squad car and said, "This is mid-July. It must be over one hundred degrees in the car!" He said, "Not to worry, the engine is running with the air conditioner set to a comfortable temperature, and I even put music on for him so that he would be calm and comfortable!" He also added, "That's a well-trained, beautiful dog. If you ever can't keep him for whatever reason, I want him." I must admit at that moment I was tempted to let the officer take him. It was hard for me to accept how easy it would be for someone to come in and walk away with my dog. Though his presence alone was generally a deterrent, clearly, a watchdog JT would never be. Good thing we have an alarm system. (Everything turned out to be fine. My husband had the alarm pad in his pocket and had accidentally set the alarm off. Needless to say, we've been very careful with it ever since.)

Whatever JT was or wasn't, we loved him very much and grieved deeply when we lost him to Wobbler's Disease at the age of six. For several months I found it very difficult to sit at the piano. I would sit down to play and could almost sense his presence with me. I'd remember vividly how it felt to have his head in my lap or his body lying on my feet as I tried to work the pedals while playing. After he was gone, it hurt not to have him there with me. Mozart was put away for a season as my tears fell on the piano keys—tears of joy for having had him and tears of sorrow at losing him at such a young age. Both are natural when you lose family.

Chapter 4

House of Two Brothers— Rocky and Rowdy

(Rocky) CH Teraden's Came A Cavalier
(Rowdy) CH Teraden's Crimson Cavalier

Rocky

Rowdy

"**I**t's a Doberman or nothing," was Terry Lee's position when his family decided they wanted to get a dog. That was almost fifty years ago and they have never looked back. I couldn't help but wonder if most of us who have Dobermans got them for the same reason. They are smart, clean, good watchdogs, short haired, short tailed, trustworthy, loyal, and very entertaining! I met Jennifer Lee, Terry's daughter, about thirty-seven years ago when she was recommended to me as an excellent junior handler at the time I was showing Rischa. I didn't know at the time how often our lives, as related to our dogs, would intersect from that time forward.

One of Jennifer's earliest dog memories was of a family trip they took to the beach. Jennifer was probably seven years old at the time and her sister Andi was five. California has many dog friendly beaches so of course they took their dog Rommel (CH Weichardt's Rosen Cavalier CD) with them. Unfortunately, what they didn't know and realized too late was that the beach they had selected was a clothing optional beach. So they stepped onto the beach and came face-to-face with a gentleman whose lady friend was sitting on his shoulders. With absolutely not a stitch of clothing on, this gentleman found himself standing in front of a ninety pound Doberman. I'm sure the last thing he wanted was this dog sniffing him anywhere but with someone on your shoulders, running was not an option and probably would have been unwise anyway. A tactical retreat was called for. The gentleman carefully backed away and the Lees decided they should probably choose another locale for their adventure that day.

I'm convinced that dogs have a sense of humor, and I bet if Rommel could have talked, he would have thought this situation was really funny. It was a short day at the beach but there would be many more adventures to come. Rommel, who took Best in Show at the Cow Palace in 1973, was a foundation dog for many of the Teraden Champions that would come after him.

After that, the Lee household was seldom short of dogs that enjoyed their secondary jobs as gatekeepers. Their first job of course was to be played with, petted until they couldn't stand it (they can stand quite a bit; I know this from experience), to be spoiled, and loved very much. They lived inside with the Lees so sometimes if one was going to the Lee house unannounced, they may have found themselves being met by the Doberman gang.

There was one such occasion when Jennifer was dating a young man. He came to the gate, saw no one, and so entered into the yard and knocked on their front door. His knocking was apparently not heard because no one answered. However, he did find himself surrounded by seven Dobermans. Either Rocky or Rowdy was among the group. (The two were seldom if ever together as two adult males because they would fight.) I asked Jennifer if the young man ever asked her out again and to his credit, he did. That's guts!

Rocky and Rowdy were litter brothers, both beautiful dogs, but as different as night and day to me. Jennifer described Rocky as a black, devoted dog with a true Doberman temperament while Rowdy was a red, happy-go-lucky, fun-loving, tug-of-war-happy dog. I saw Rocky as reserved, stately and elegant. I would see him out in the yard, and this dog would actually stack himself. Stacking is a term used to describe positioning a dog while he's standing, in a manner that exhibits his best physical attributes. A lot of dogs do that on their own sometimes, but Rocky seemed to me to be a master of it.

When Rocky came to say "hi" to me and be petted, he would virtually glide seamlessly. There was a time I wondered if he could teach me to do that—very classy. In contrast, I remember the first time I met Rowdy. As soon as I was welcomed, Rowdy was pouncing around in front of me with a ball as if to say, "Let's go play. I'm ready!" I didn't move fast enough so he picked up the ball and dropped it on my feet. When I took the liberty of sitting down on a patio chair, he got the ball again and dropped it into my lap with a great big tail-wagging "woof" added to the mix. This was a dog that could communicate. You knew exactly what he wanted—no second guessing here.

I read a book about Boxers recently that talked about how Boxers are known to "clown around," but I'm saying no dog I'd ever met prior to that time knew how to clown around any better than Rowdy. And I loved him for it. I thought that people who were afraid of Dobermans should be introduced to Rowdy. He was able to sense the environment around him so well, and if there was no threat, he could make anyone feel comfortable. It was a gift. In the world of Dobermans, Rowdy would have won "Mr. Congeniality."

That doesn't mean that Rocky and Rowdy weren't protective. Jennifer told me of the time she took Rocky and Rowdy to be temperament tested to evaluate whether or not they demonstrated the protective instinct for which the Doberman breed was intended. They both passed everything except the agitation portion. The reason given was that both dogs stayed at her side instead of going out to the end of the leash when the agitator approached.

That night Jennifer, along with her mother, Denyse, had brought with them Jennifer's then seven- or eight-month-old son, Nick, who was in a stroller. While the dogs were being tested, Nick stayed with Denyse, but when they were done, Jennifer was pushing Nick's stroller and had Rocky with her on leash. Just as they were leaving, Bob, another Doberman owner started walking toward them. When Bob approached to where he was about a foot and a half away, Rocky alerted and watched him. But the minute Bob touched Nick's stroller, Rocky immediately protected Nick and decisively let Bob know that he was not under any circumstances to touch the stroller. Clearly, when Rocky was being tested, he didn't sense any threat to Jennifer, but when Nick's personal space boundary was crossed by a stranger, Rocky went into action. Bob jumped back and Rocky relaxed. Very appropriate.

I've never known Rowdy, Mr. Personality, to be self-conscious. One year at one of the annual dog shows held in Carmel, California, Jennifer was in the Conformation ring showing a client's dog. Denyse had Rowdy on leash, and they were standing by a tree about fifteen feet from the ring. Denyse clearly had her focus on Jennifer and the dog she was showing and wasn't attentive to Rowdy who was apparently pacing around, hinting that he needed to take a bathroom break. As Denyse continued to remain temporarily oblivious to Rowdy, a man walked over to her and said, "Ma'am, are you aware that your dog just backed up to your purse and took care of his business in it?" When Denyse turned around and looked down at her purse, sure enough, there was a Doberman-sized pile of poop in it. There are just some occasions when a poop pick-up bag is not quite enough to adequately address the need. I am glad that I'm not the only one whose dog occasionally embarrasses mom!

With Rowdy, there was never a dull moment. One year, Jennifer was showing Rowdy at a Specialty show just before the Nationals. Besides Rowdy, there were about twelve or thirteen other dogs in the class. Rowdy was showing very well, standing in about the middle of the group, when Jennifer started preparing him for his turn to be judged. Just about the time the judge was getting to him, everyone could hear sirens approaching nearby. Jennifer, knowing Rowdy's propensity to howl when he heard sirens, tried nonchalantly to put her hand on Rowdy's mouth. About this time, the judge turned to Jennifer and said, "Please remove your hand from your dog's mouth." Jennifer of course did as was requested, and the minute she did, Rowdy threw his head back and began to howl. It didn't take but a few seconds before many of the other dogs in the ring joined in the joyful chorus. This must have been an exciting performance because before it was over, dogs in other rings and even dogs in adjacent buildings got into the fun. Needless to say, that Specialty show turned out to be a howling success. Incidentally, Rowdy was awarded first place.

Rocky also did very well in the show ring finishing at an early age. Jennifer continued showing him long after he was a champion. At one particular Doberman Pinscher National Specialty show, she was showing him in the Best of Breed class. As the judging concluded, the judge was going down the line and handing out some Awards of Merit. The dog ahead of Rocky received one and Jennifer was ready to reach out and receive one for Rocky when to her dismay the judge passed her by. Fighting the urge to cry, Jennifer just wanted to finish and get out of the ring to hide her dis-appointment—until the judge turned to announce that the Best of Breed would go to a lovely red female, and Rocky, at the age of eight, went Best Opposite Sex. Very impressive.

One of the most memorable events for the Lees came when they were approached with the story that there was going to be a memorial erected in Guam for military dogs that had lost their lives in service for their country. The statue would be of a Doberman because it was a Doberman that was the first to die in the line of duty. Susan Bahary-Wilner was commissioned to do the sculpture that would be entitled "Always Faithful," and she needed an excellent representative of the breed to be the model for the memorial. Rowdy was chosen for this honor.

But the much greater story is of the dogs that the statue represents. The statue was dedicated on July 21, 1994. On one side of the statue the inscription reads: "'Always Faithful' was inspired by the spirit of these heroic dogs who are the embodiment of love and devotion." To honor the working heritage of the Doberman Pinscher, the United Doberman Club dedicated this statue to the courageous Doberman Pinscher that valiantly served during the war in the Pacific. The other side of the statue reads, "Twenty-five Marine War Dogs gave their lives liberating Guam in 1944. They served as sentries, messengers, scouts. They explored caves, detected mines and booby traps." The dogs are then listed by name. "Given in their memory and on behalf of the surviving men of the 2nd and 3rd Marine Dog Platoons, many of whom owe their lives to the bravery and sacrifice of these gallant animals. By William W. Putney DVM C.O. 3rd Dog Platoon. Dedicated this day, 21 July 1944."

Rocky and Rowdy represented the breed well, and they live on in their sons and daughters that came after them. I hope you enjoy meeting a few of them in the stories to follow.

Always Faithful

Chapter 5

Robin

Teraden's Rockin' Robin

Robin was a Rowdy daughter that was meant to be part of our family. I had taken a friend of ours to Concord to visit the Lees who had Teraden Dobermans because he was looking for a dog. While they were talking business, I was busy playing with Rowdy who I thought was one of the coolest and most fun dogs ever. I was busy minding my own business. Rowdy had sired a litter with lots of males but only two females, that were at the time six months old, both of which the Lees were keeping.

Robin, one of the two female puppies, was also minding my business, because the more I played with Rowdy, the more determined she was to get into the action. She was a ball fiend like her dad and also apparently inherited his sense of humor. And we played. When we were through playing, Robin backed up in front of me and demanded that I pet her. By the time it was time to leave, Robin and I had developed a rapport that was unmistakable, and Denyse asked me if I wanted her. Her question came so out of the blue, I didn't know what to say. I wanted to say, "YES!" but for once I exercised some discretion and decided I'd better talk this over with my family first. So I took pictures and a little video clip of Robin, and all the way home I was thinking of a way to convince my family that I had fallen in love with this puppy and desperately wanted to bring her home. As it turned out, it didn't take much convincing. A few minutes after my family saw her pictures and the video clip, they were asking me when I could go pick her up.

We had an old red male Doberman named Sonny at the time. He was starting to slow down and act his age until I brought Robin home. For the first few minutes, both Sonny and Robin did a lot of barking at each other. They were of course both on leash during introductions so it was all talk. And then it seemed like Sonny came to his senses and likely said to himself, "This is a very cute little redhead come to keep me company, why am I complaining?" Peace was made very quickly, and in the weeks and months that followed

Robin brought such life back into Sonny. This uppity young redhead was exactly what Sonny needed as a friend and fellow trouble-maker. Robin kept Sonny feeling young and vital much longer than he otherwise would have felt, and Robin mourned him when he died.

The rest was history. Robin fit in so well with our family from the start. She was already six months old so she had great inside manners and she would come, sit, and lay down. "Stay," along with some other skills needed work, so I took her to obedience class. Robin was such a joy to work with.

At that time, Erick and I already owned our home inspection business and had an office about ten minutes from home. I often had to work some nights, so I started taking Robin with me. All I wanted from her was for her to get comfortable with being my companion and be at ease in the car, in the office, or wherever I took her. To my surprise, even at such a young age, Robin was an exceptionally good watchdog. That was most unexpected. No one came near the office without her knowing about it. After hours, people seldom came to our office door, but when they did, they would find themselves face-to-face with Robin.

Robin was a small dog for a Doberman, but when you looked in her eyes, you knew that when it was needed, she was all business. I found that unique for a puppy, but then I remembered that she'd been hanging around with her dad and the other adult Dobermans. What I saw in her when she wasn't being protective was a sweet, funny, little red girl, absolutely full of fun.

In our office we had a relatively long hallway leading from the front door and offices to the main workroom. Though I didn't usually have Robin with me at the office during the normal workday, there were times when I would have her with me, especially if I was just stopping by. On one such day, work was slow and most everyone was enjoying Robin's presence. One of the inspectors and I were playing a game of keep-away from Robin with a small football. Every few tosses I made sure to let her get it if she hadn't already on her own. Believe me, Robin could get just about anything away from anybody when she put her mind to it. She was such a strong and enthusiastic little lady.

Several minutes into this game, I had just caught the football and Robin was already back in front of me when she went for the ball. Unfortunately, my fingers were still holding the ball when Robin's jaw clamped down on it. I screamed, "Ouch!" and Robin immediately released the ball, looked at me, and realized I was hurt. I sat down and Robin was in my lap licking my tears and whimpering as if to say, "I am so sorry. I didn't mean to hurt you!" Of course she didn't. We were playing a game, and I simply didn't let go quickly enough. Accidents happen. I went to the hospital to get my broken finger fixed up, and Robin played nurse for me for several days thereafter. She was constantly by my side, which was very sweet, but also very annoying after a while until I convinced her that I was better. This dog had such a tender heart, not only for me but also for my family.

Robin definitely had her mannerisms that made her uniquely her. Not that other dogs don't have some of the same mannerisms, but Robin exhibited them in a way that was just her. I remember the way she would sit on the stairs and soak up the sun coming through our expansive windows, the way she would lay on her back for belly-rubs, and the cowlick on her nose that tickled when she bopped your hand when she thought you hadn't petted her enough. And of course, her affinity for playing ball. I used to say that Robin would play ball till the cows came home, maybe even longer if she could get away with it.

Robin was definitely unique. One day I came home from the office to find Robin on my front porch sunning herself, at perfect peace with one front paw crossed over the other. Robin was always kept safely secured in the house when I was gone so I couldn't even imagine how she got out. To this day, I don't know what happened, but my neighbor from across the way said she saw Robin out front, but that she never left our yard and settled by the front door. I'd bet that was one day when we didn't have a single door-to-door solicitor. When I got out of my car, Robin calmly yawned, stretched, and pawed at the door as if to say, "It's about time you got home, I'm ready for a snack and a nap."

"Waiting for the ball"

Living with Robin was a continuous adventure. I had begun studying martial arts after Robin came to live with us. I could count on Robin to always greet me at the door when I came home. One night I had just walked in the house, my family was in the living room watching a television program, and though I noticed Robin hadn't greeted me, I got caught up in the program and didn't look to see where Robin was. Not more than a few minutes later, I was lying on the couch watching the program and Robin came over to me and nuzzled her face against me. I took a glance at her and then took another good long look. Have you ever seen something and thought, *Okay, what's wrong with this picture*? Finally, I said aloud, "Why does my dog have a pink muzzle?" There was a beat of absolute silence until my daughter, Erin, blurted out, "The cake!!!" She ran into the kitchen to discover that about three-fourths of the strawberry cake that she had recently finished baking and frosting was gone. Robin's entire muzzle almost up to her eyes was covered in strawberry cake crumbs and frosting. Miss Robin, we discovered, was a natural counter surfer. Though the cake had been pushed well into a corner, she got up there and helped herself to several days' worth of dessert. Not even her dessert. Wish I had thought to get a picture of her before I cleaned her up. Talk about a Kodak moment.

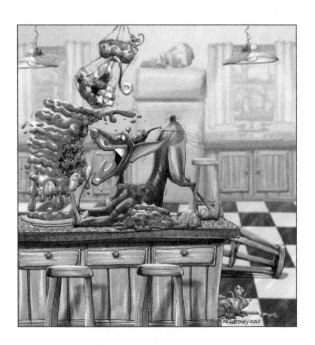

What I probably appreciated least about Robin, if there could be such a thing, was that she was a hunter extraordinaire. We have an excellent enclosure all the way around our yard and Robin took great exception to anyone or anything coming into it uninvited. The good thing was that if it was a person, she merely held them at bay until I came out to investigate. But we would often get birds, cats, possum, and squirrels that would get into our yard, and then the fight was on.

However, in writing this story, I was reminded that when I brought Robin home, my daughter, Erin, had a cat named Hannibal. And Erin thought that despite Robin's hatred for cats, she tolerated Hannibal's presence in the house for a few days extremely graciously until Hannibal went to his new home. But otherwise, no exceptions.

Robin was amazing. Once she even caught a bird that was in mid-flight. The bird was flying low, but still, what timing! If I hadn't seen it for myself, I'm not sure I would have believed it. Apparently, Robin inherited this trait from her mother, not from Rowdy, but dealing with it was a challenge. I often rescued cats from her jaws and would call Animal Control to come get them if I didn't know where the cat lived. In fact, Animal Control took injured possums and birds as well.

Probably the most challenging incident occurred with our next door neighbor's chicken. We have the most wonderful neighbors anyone could ask for. They moved into their home about the same time we moved into ours and we enjoyed living next door to them. Then they got a chicken. I didn't have any problem with it and really neither did Robin until the chicken started to fly up onto the fence separating our yards. I could see trouble coming, so I suggested to our neighbors that it might be wise to clip the chicken's wings so as to keep it off the fence. But day after day the chicken was up on the fence clucking at Robin. Robin took serious exception to that, and I could see her waiting for her opportunity to put the chicken in her place. I wasn't sure what to do, but Robin was safely protected inside when we weren't home anyway, so I wasn't too worried and figured I could protect the chicken when I was home.

Good in theory until one day my kids got home from school before I got home from work and they let Robin out. Without the chicken, this would not have been a problem. But I got a call at the office, "Mom, Robin's out and we can't get her back." I made it home in record time to find that Robin had knocked a board loose in the fence and was in our neighbor's yard running amok. She was halfway up her sides in mud with chicken feathers sticking out of her muzzle and feathers also stuck to the mud all over her. Our neighbors were powerless to stop her. What a mess—the dog, the yard, everything. I called Robin and thank goodness she immediately came. I had the kids bathe her, and I went to talk with my neighbors.

I looked at them standing on their back porch, and as I approached, they lifted something up to show me. I said, "What is that?" "That" was all that was left of the chicken.

Except for the feet and the beak, it was utterly unrecogniz-able as ever having been a chicken. The closest thing I could relate it to would be the rubber chickens that fans used to hang out at the Giants ballpark when the opposing team wouldn't pitch to Barry Bonds. This chicken should have looked so good. I apologized to my neighbors profusely, offered to clean up the yard, replace the chicken, whatever I could do to make amends. So there was peace. And they weren't mad at Robin as I assumed that they would be and even took responsibility for their chicken taunting her. I was so blessed for a peaceful resolution. However, at our house, the chicken jokes were the rage for days. "Couldn't Robin have waited for KFC?" Or, "Robin must have been in a fowl mood!"

Robin was absolutely wonderful with other people and other dogs, especially in public. At home, nobody came in unless Erick and I were there to let them in. Once they were invited in, she was calm and loving while remaining attentive. She was always protective of my kids. A visitor, whether they were friend or extended family, could not yell at my kids or make sudden moves toward them without Robin "speaking up" and positioning herself between them. And everyone knew that Robin meant it. At the same time, she was infinitely patient with little ones, which was some-what surprising since my kids were already either in junior high school or high school when Robin came to live with us. When our grandson, Joshua, was born, Robin was protec-tive of him but so gentle and tolerant of the new addition to our family, even later when he occasionally took her toys or laid on her more firmly than was comfortable.

My Aunt Carmen lived in Monterey, which is about an hour and a half south of us. We always invited her to visit, especially for special events and she *really* liked Robin.

After Carmen suffered a major stroke that necessitated her being admitted into a convalescent hospital, I would go down regularly and visit her, as well as make sure that all her needs were met. After she had made some improvement in her condition, she would ask me to bring Robin for a visit. I told her that I didn't think the care facility would allow it, but she persisted until I told her I would ask. So I did. They asked me what kind of a dog I had, and I said as sweetly as I could, "A Doberman." Can you guess what they told me? "Absolutely not!" I explained to them how much Carmen loved Robin and asked if we could maybe arrange in advance to just bring Carmen out in front of the facility in her wheelchair and Robin (on leash) could see her there? To my surprise, they agreed, and I brought Robin down at the appointed time.

My aunt was so incredibly happy to see her but an unforeseeable and unexpected problem developed. Some of the other residents saw Carmen with Robin through the big picture window in the front of the building and decided they wanted to visit with Robin too. This seemed to frustrate the facility staff to no end. I thought it was funny but very wisely didn't say so. Eventually, Robin had quite a following. After Robin died, I received sympathy cards from patients and staff alike who remembered how much Robin enriched their lives with just her sweet presence.

During the time I had Robin, I went through a very difficult season in my life. I am blessed with great family and friends, but Robin was the one who was with me continually. I told her everything. She listened without judgment, laid her head in my lap and comforted me, never gossiped about me, and no matter what kind of day I had, she greeted me with such excitement. One would think she hadn't seen me in a week rather than a few hours or even a few minutes.

I am convinced that if anyone needs or wants a boost in their self-esteem, they should get a good dog.

Robin was always in the middle of whatever the family was doing. When we came home from work or school, she was always ready to play. One night, I had just come home from my martial arts class and my son, Michael, and I started talking and tossing treats to Robin. We were having fun. As it was getting late, Michael went to bed, and I went to take my shower after an evening of rigorous training. Robin's favorite place to lie down was on a small landing where there was a turn in our stairs. She could see everything going on from there. Our ritual was that after my shower, I would go downstairs to get fresh water for the night. Our house has a lot of windows and natural light so I wouldn't have to turn on any lights to be able to see well. When I would get to the landing, I would gently step over Robin and she would push her nose against me as if to say, "You cannot pass by here without stopping to pet me." And of course I would stop and give her love every time.

This particular night, as always, I stepped over Robin, but she didn't move. This didn't make sense. After calling her with no response, I frantically turned on the light and ran to my Robin, but she was gone. When I saw her fifteen minutes prior, she was perfectly well. Now my sweet Robin was gone. She was still warm, and I tried to revive her as one would a puppy that isn't breathing at birth. Then I just held her and cried my heart out. The vet said there was nothing in her system that was harmful, neither was there any evidence of injury. Her heart had just stopped. After all that Robin and I had been through together, for a while it felt like mine had too.

Chapter 6

Jack

BISS AM/CAN CH Anozira's Cactus Jack SchH-3, FH,
IPO-3, WH, AD, CDX, NAJ, RE, CAN CD, ROMC, ROM

I asked my friend Jean Boland if she believed in love at first sight. I was not surprised that she replied with an emphatic "yes." I thought she might, especially after she described to me her trip to Arizona in August of 1995 to pick out her new puppy. Jack was a red male Doberman, one of five male puppies in a lovely litter. Jean actually had her eye on a different puppy, but this little red male obviously had his eye on her, since he kept going to her and wanting to stay with her. Jean came to believe that this puppy she named Jack was meant to be hers; certainly Jack somehow knew this, and from then on Jean's adventure, living with Jack, began.

The first thing that endeared Jack and his story to me was that Jack and Robin were so closely related. As you know from having read their story, Jack's father, Rocky, and Robin's father, Rowdy, were litter brothers. Having known both brothers well, I felt that alone told me a lot about what

Jack may have been like. Though from all I had heard about Jack, he seemed to me to have inherited his temperament and personality from his Uncle Rowdy rather than from his dad, and as I share his story, I think my reasoning will become evident.

Jean describes Jack as being "wicked smart." From the time he was very young, Jack loved to learn anything and everything new. That makes training a lot of fun and much easier. Jack earned many of his obedience titles at a relatively young age. Probably the greatest thing about having a well-trained dog is that it's possible to take the dog almost anywhere and have the dog be welcome. Jean's dogs, like mine, are family, and our trips are most fun when the dogs can come along without issue.

One of Jacks favorite things to do in obedience was to retrieve, and one of the skills in an obedience Open class is the retrieve over the high jump. Since Jack loved to retrieve, he met the challenge of this exercise with great exuberance. In the Open class, the handler and dog stand back in front of the jump by a certain number of feet; the handler throws the dumbbell, then sends the dog over the jump to retrieve it, and the dog should then return back over the same jump with the dumbbell.

Photo by Daybreak Design
Photography

Once when Jack was competing in the Open

class at an AKC trial, he was so excited in getting the opportunity to retrieve, he didn't wait to be sent and excitedly took off over the jump as Jean was starting to throw the dumbbell. Jack was fast! He beat the dumbbell over the jump, and probably wondered momentarily where it went. But when he saw it, he did proudly return over the jump with the dumbbell in his mouth. (Jack be nimble, Jack be quick!) Though Jack was disqualified for leaving Jean's side without being sent, if I'd been judging, after I stopped laughing, I would probably have been tempted to give Jack extra points for being able to make adjustments when things didn't go as planned. Besides, he was obviously having fun. There are few things more beautiful in the world of working dogs than to watch one perform who absolutely loves to work and it shows in every fiber of his being.

Jack made friends wherever he went. One day that was very memorable, Jean had taken Jack to his Schutzund class. Schutzund is a German working title made up of three components, one third tracking, one third obedience, and one third protection. A dog must excel in all three areas to earn his title. So one night at class, before it was Jack's turn to perform, Jean had him crated in the car with the hatchback open. When Jack's turn came, Jean went to get him and found a friend's four-year-old daughter, Heather, feeding Jack cookies. When

Jack in Schutzund Trial

Jean asked Heather what she was doing, she calmly replied, "Jack and I are having a picnic." Like it was the most natural thing in the world.

Thursday nights were Jack's regular obedience training nights. Since Jean works full time, it was hard to find time to get something to eat. So they would often stop at a particular Burger King, go through the drive through, and enjoy eating as they went on their way. Since this was a regular stop for Jean and Jack, the manager at Burger King got to know them very well. Jack must have been very lovable, because after a time, the manager would expect their visit and not only have Jean's order, but have whole hamburgers waiting for Jack. As soon as Jean stopped at the drive-up window, Jack would jump over her lap and stick his head out of her driver's side window waiting for his burger! And if they didn't come quickly enough, Jack would start barking, which must have echoed throughout the restaurant. It was as if Jack was saying, "I am here . . . hello!" I can imagine what a funny sight that must have been, Jack barking for his burgers. He was certainly a go get 'em guy!

From all that I've heard and learned about Jack, I think one of the things that I appreciate most about him is his obvious sense of humor. It's wonderful to have a smart dog or, as Jean described it, a "wicked smart" dog, but it can be a challenge when your dog sometimes thinks one step ahead of you and you're trying to keep up. Dogs like this seem to think they can handle things for themselves and are ready to take advantage of opportunities that arise. This can take many different forms. For instance, if you're at a dog show and don't happen to have the dog's drinking bowl available, then follow Jack's example and jump up on the drinking fountain intended for people and help yourself. For Jack, it didn't stop there. Once when his sweet tooth had him thinking about treats, Jack tried to steal a doughnut from a lady in a wheelchair. Had he succeeded, I'm sure he would have sweetly expressed his gratitude, and though he was unsuccessful that time, I doubt he quit trying when other opportunities arose.

Jack was even more inventive at home. He figured out how to open doors regardless of what type of door handle was used. Jack opened the round doorknobs that pull in to open by putting his mouth over the doorknob, twisting, and pulling it in to open. It could be unnerving to find that your dog can open the bathroom door that you've just shut hoping for a little privacy. Jean was certainly surprised when Jack would just open the bedroom door that she secured, so he could enjoy the comfort of her bed. Sometimes he also had other ulterior motives such as to search for his birthday or Christmas presents, which, by the way, Jack was perfectly capable of opening by himself.

Jack opening bedroom door

Living on some acreage, Jean finds that she sometimes has trouble with field mice in the basement. Jack decided to pronounce himself watchdog against these mice; after all, this was his home to protect. Problem was, the door to the basement was shut, and it had a round doorknob that pushes out to open and swings into the basement. Hmmm . . . okay, after some thought, no problem. Jack discovered that he could open this type of doorknob by standing on his back legs, body weight on the door, pawing the doorknob until it twisted to the right spot, and then his body weight pushed the door open. Once he obtained access, Jack took the dog blanket that Jean had carefully folded and stacked down into the basement and laid down comfortably to watch for field mice. That's exactly how Jean found him once. I asked Jean what she did when she found him like that, and she said, "I laughed! His intelligence, determination, and creativity were absolutely amazing!"

Jack was a dog who firmly believed in developing and honing his talents. Once he had doorknobs mastered, he graduated to cupboard doors. If he wanted his rawhide chews from the cupboard, it was almost as if he said to Jean, "Don't trouble yourself, I can get this!" Eventually Jean had to install baby locks on all cabinets and doors, since Jack had been able to pretty much gain access to whatever he wanted. And not just at his home. Jack could flip up the cookie jar lid at the vet's. I wonder how many other dogs saw him do this and said to themselves, "I wonder how he learned to do that . . . maybe going to the vet might not be so bad, at least it's not without its perks."

Food was not always the motivation. Jack also took delight in finding Jean's keys for her. I know a lot of people who would appreciate their dog developing that skill. A little more unusual skill was that Jack would grab tissues for Jean if she said, "Achoo!" I'm not sure that I would want to use a tissue that has been in a dog's mouth but how could anybody resist his sweetness in being so helpful?! I'd probably pretend to sneeze just for the entertainment value.

Don't let Jack's obvious comedic personality fool you. He could be all business when necessary. Jean lives on a three-and-a-half acre lot that has a one-hundred foot driveway. One night, during the winter as Jean was coming home from work, she stopped at the front of the driveway to get her mail. Even from that long distance, she could hear Jack and his daughter Jill barking. Jack was loose in the house, and it was not common for him to be carrying on that way since they don't have close neighbors and normal traffic going by. And the dogs knew the sounds of her approaching and didn't normally bark. As Jean got back in her car to drive toward the house, she saw a man coming toward her on a bike. It was pitch black out, but the dogs knew he was there and warned Jean of the potential threat.

Jean would take Jack hiking in the Adirondacks where they could just enjoy the day by the lake and then hike back. On one such trip, Jean and Jack saw a truck that was left at the trailhead with an empty gun rack. She figured that more than likely the owner of that truck, potentially with friends, was on the trail ahead. Not entirely sure as to the wisdom of her decision, she proceeded with the hike as planned. She had come too far to turn back without real cause. She and Jack took off on their hike, and as it happened they did encounter three armed men who claimed they were hunting bear. It was certainly a plausible explanation but Jean was very glad that she had Jack by her side.

Jean would often, if not always, take Jack with her when she went hiking or just for a walk. In the area where she lives, and really in many rural areas especially, it is common courtesy to acknowledge people passing by. Jean generally made a practice of being courteous to whomever she met. Occasionally such courtesies may be misinterpreted.

On one particular walk, Jean and Jack were already on their way home when a car went past. Jean, as usual, raised a hand up in a courteous acknowledgement of the driver. However in this case, Jean could hear the car slowing down and much to her dismay, the driver turned around and pulled up next to them. The driver then tried to strike up a conversation and as he did, Jean pulled Jack up close beside her already thinking ahead about what she may have to deal with. In the process, the driver asked Jean, "Does your dog bite?" Jean now perceiving a potential threat, responded with, "Any dog will bite," likely thinking to herself, *under the right circumstances*. Regardless, the driver, seeing Jack, obviously decided that he wasn't interested in finding out whether Jack would bite or not and wisely drove on.

In all my years studying martial arts and street self-defense, one of the many things that I learned is that the best fight is the one you can either avoid completely or walk away from before the situation escalates. A woman by herself out for a walk, especially in a relatively low traffic area, can appear to be an easy target whether it's true or not, but a woman walking with an eighty pound, alert Doberman would make most anyone think twice about starting any altercation. When I asked Jean about Jack's response in potentially confrontational situations, she said that Jack was really good at discriminating between when a situation was a legitimate threat and when it wasn't.

I had often heard Jack referred to as "the lizard boy," and how Jack was keeping New York free of lizards. When I asked Jean about it, she said that actually there are no lizards in New York and not because of Jack, and that the "lizard boy" reference was a creative idea for one of Jack's ad campaigns in a Doberman magazine and somehow it stuck. However, apparently Jack's father, Rocky, as well as his grandmother, were the real deal; they loved to chase lizards. So, without initially knowing it, Jack came by that nickname honestly. And whether or not, Jack had opportunities to chase after those lizards, he must have carried the gene, because he passed it on to Kobe, and I have to believe he likely passed it on to many more of his offspring.

Jean describes Jack as always being a happy boy that made her laugh every single day. Jack lived life to its fullest every day and showed Jean what aging gracefully is all about. Jack was a wonderful ambassador for the Doberman breed. He was the third Doberman ever to earn his American Championship and his Schutzund 3 title in the history of the breed. This was clear evidence of not only his excellence as a specimen of the breed but his exceptional working ability. He exemplified the best of Doberman temperament—smart, protective, loving, and loyal. Jack died in November of 2009, at the age of fourteen. But Jack lives on through his puppies, many of whom are imprinted with Jack's elegance, "wicked smart" trainability, love of adventure, and as in Kobe's case, also Jack's sense of humor. Jack will always remain in the hearts of many as one of the breed's more memorable dogs.

Best Veteran Dog—2002 DPCA National Sweepstakes

Jack Tracking—Photo by Daybreak Design Photography

Chapter 7

Kobe

Smack Dab's Knight Gekkota CGC

I want to introduce Kobe now because even at this young age, his life is intertwined with a number of the other dogs whose stories will be shared. Kobe is the second puppy in my life that I waited for based on pedigree. I wanted a smart, loving, naturally protective dog with a proven working pedigree, solid temperament, and of course a sense of humor. Kobe does not disappoint.

One night months before I even heard of an available quality litter of puppies, I was watching a Laker's game on television, and during the half-time show, the commentators were discussing why Kobe Bryant, nicknamed in the NBA "the black mamba" is such an excellent basketball player. Among others things, they said that Kobe is smart, can anticipate moves in advance, is fearless, never gives up, and loves to work. I found myself thinking that those were some of the very qualities I was looking for in my new puppy and that Kobe would be an excellent call name for him.

The right litter came along in May of 2011, and seven weeks later I went to Chicago to pick out my puppy. I was blessed to be allowed a lot of time playing with and watching all the puppies. It didn't take me long to realize that choosing a puppy from this litter would not be an easy task. All the puppies were lovely, good tempered, and fun loving.

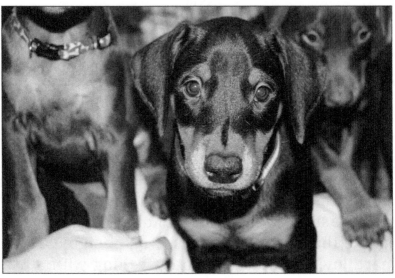

Kobe at 7 weeks

In the room adjacent to the puppy room, there was a large table with chairs in the center of the room. About midafternoon of my second day there, several of the puppies were playing and chasing each other around, over and under the chair leg rungs, and I found myself imagining these puppies as working dogs and thought, "I can't go wrong no matter which puppy I pick." That's when it happened. Several of the puppies were playing, tumbling all over each other with a little black male with a blue collar at the bottom of the pile. He didn't seem to mind being there, tolerated it for a while as it was all in good fun, but the point came when he had had enough. He somehow managed to wriggle his way out of the pile, got up, turned to face the others and, very convincingly I might add, told them to "knock it off." A ninety pound Doberman barking and growling can sound very menacing, but at seven weeks this little guy taking his stand was absolutely adorable. Then he went right on playing as if nothing had happened. This was a puppy of character. It was then I knew that this little black male was the puppy for me, and Kobe became part of our family.

One day when Kobe was about eleven weeks old, I took him to the vet for one of his routine puppy shots. I was in the waiting room and there was a couple waiting for their dog's treatment to be completed. As I sat there, they noticed Kobe and how cute he was even with his taped ears and asked me about him. As we were chatting, a lady came in with three dogs that were semi-out-of-control and they began barking at Kobe. Kobe may be a Doberman but at that time he was a very young and very little Doberman who clearly didn't think that taking on three dogs who were not that big, but all were certainly bigger and older than he was, was such a good idea. So Kobe wedged himself under the bench and between my ankles and peered out. I continued to talk with the couple, and the husband asked me what my puppy's name was. So I said, "Kobe," but he didn't understand me clearly and asked, "Do you spell that C-o-l-b-y?" And I said, "Actually, no, it's K-o-b-e." "Oh, like Kobe Bryant?" he asked. "Yes, exactly!" I replied. "Doesn't he look like 'the black mamba' to you?" Trying hard not to chuckle, the husband said, "The way he's peeking out from between your ankles, no not really." I told them, "That's okay, give him a year or two!"

From very early on, Kobe reminded me that he was Jack's son. One day, when Kobe was four months old, I crated him in his soft travelling crate while I was busy and couldn't watch him. We have a home office and I was taking care of business when I looked down and to my chagrin, there was Kobe. "How in the world did you get out?" I asked him. Not that he could answer. He just looked at me so cute and so smug. So I re-crated Kobe, pretended to work, but out of my peripheral vision, I watched and waited. I didn't have to wait long to see Kobe repeatedly paw at the zipper and with those cute little puppy teeth pull on the zipper until he could push his head through the opening and out he came. I saw it and still was not inclined to believe it. I sat there watching him and wondered what in the world I'd gotten myself into.

Kobe grew faster than I would have thought possible, and I started his obedience training early. When puppies are tiny and sweet and they run over you, it's cute. When they get to be seventy pounds or more and they run over you, it's not so cute anymore. I had learned this from previous experience, and I'm pleased to say Kobe has grown up for the most part a real gentleman. Kobe grew quickly, but despite his rapid growth, he still definitely looked like a puppy.

Kobe at 14 months

One day as I was cooking dinner, the doorbell rang and of course Kobe jumped up on the couch that was positioned in front of our bay window and barked, clearly (in his mind) trying to convince our caller that entering without invitation was inadvisable. I answered the door and found it was a salesperson from an alarm company hoping to sell us a home alarm system. We talked only for a few minutes as I told him we already had an alarm system. As he looked at Kobe through the window, he said, "Yes, I can see that." I said, "No, I mean we have a real in-home alarm system." As we talked a minute more, he kept looking from me to Kobe and back and forth again. Finally he said, "That is the biggest Doberman I have ever seen!" To which I replied, "He's only seven months old and he really isn't that big, not yet anyway; he's just standing on the couch." I was trying hard to keep a straight face as the gentleman thanked me for my time and slowly backed off my front porch. Kobe must have more of a commanding presence than I thought. What a good boy.

Kobe, even at his young age, will definitely let us know if someone is coming. He always barks if there is something requiring our attention and doesn't bark without cause. Kobe has a very stable temperament and has been very good with people we invite in to our home. Home or away from home, he's great with people, kids, dogs, even cats for the most part. He's been well socialized. Though I shouldn't have been, I was surprised by his reaction to an incident that occurred when Kobe was about eight months old.

I had taken Kobe out to the park for an afternoon walk, and we were already on our way back to the car. I saw a man approaching us, someone I had taken note of before, because he was the only one out there consistently without any apparent purpose. Everyone else at the park was walking, picnicking, or doing some other activity, but every time I saw this man, he was just standing at his car watching. So I was always careful to keep my distance. That day as Kobe and I were almost back to my car, this man closed his distance to us, and I turned to face him. It's always unwise to turn your back on a potential threat. I had pulled Kobe very close to me on my left side as I was trying to figure out what this guy wanted. The man started telling me how beautiful my dog was, how he'd been watching us. It somehow didn't have the sound of a compliment to me. He then asked to pet my dog, which I normally don't have a problem with. But something about this guy didn't feel right so I said," I'm sorry, I'm not comfortable with that, please back off." "Oh why not?" he wanted to know as he continued to slowly approach. "I see how sweet your dog is with those kids out there."

It was then that it occurred to me that this guy might actually try to take my dog from me. Right then I was grateful for all the years of my training both in martial arts and street self-defense because I was determined to protect my puppy. I pulled Kobe even closer and this time told the guy firmly and in no uncertain terms to back off. His response was to reach out with both hands as if to grab Kobe on either side of his face. The moment he closed the distance to about three feet (too close), Kobe's fur came up the entire length of his back and he hit the end of that short lead with teeth bared. I don't know who was more surprised, the man or me. Fortunately for him and for me, he took off as I prepared to report the incident. That night Kobe got steak with his dinner . . . just kidding, but I did hug him over and over and told him he was the best dog ever and how much I loved him. Not that Kobe didn't already know that. And yes, he did get some extra treats.

I was shocked, but some weeks later, the same man showed up at the park after we were already there, this time with several of his friends. I saw them from a distance and pulled out my cell phone to call 911, but as it turned out, it was unnecessary. Kobe remembered the man from the previous incident and while still at some distance, bared his teeth and convinced him and his friends to retreat. I reported the incident anyway and have not seen them since. I have a most excellent gatekeeper!

True to his pedigree, Kobe loves to work. In fact I don't think Kobe sees training as work. In the early days of his training, I went to great lengths to convince him that working time is not the time for his antics. In the Novice class one of the skills is the figure 8. Two handlers with their dogs stand as posts about six feet apart, and the third handler with his/her dog begins to do a figure 8 around the posts while the instructor calls out heeling commands. In one of the first classes, Kobe and I were standing as a post and I had a close eye on Kobe, who was about seven months old then, because of his propensity for inviting the performing dog to play. The dog always heels on the handler's left side, so this time when they were rounding our side of the figure 8, the handler was between Kobe and her dog. She also had the treats in her right side pocket since her dog was on her left. She cut the turn a little close and before I could stop him, Kobe made a lunge for that treat bag hanging out of her pocket and stole a treat before the handler had time to react. Talk about surprised. No one ever made that mistake again.

Kobe has always found ways to enjoy class. Still in this same Novice class but on a different night, we were working on our precision in heeling. Kobe, like most puppies, had a rather limited attention span. This particular night he was more distracted than usual. In the next ring over, which was the Show Novice class, the instructor had the handlers bring toys to class in an effort to teach the dogs to work amidst distractions. At one point during our heeling exercise, the number of squeaky toys sounding in the next ring got to be too much for Kobe, because when our instructor called, "About turn," Kobe bolted and kept right on going in the same direction, directly into the next ring, determined to help himself to one of those toys. That's how he met Lora Cox, the instructor in that next ring who, thank goodness, seemed absolutely unfazed by Kobe's unexpected arrival. Of course I was right behind him. After class, I took Kobe over for an official introduction and an apology.

Obedience classes are really fun. When Kobe graduated into the Show Novice class, he remembered Lora, and I have a feeling she remembered him too. I soon saw that Kobe would not ever be able to put one over on her as she appeared to be wise to dog tricks and likely had seen it all. Seeing how she helped with Kobe, I got the impression she may actually have or have had one such as mine. From the beginning, Kobe liked her.

When I was preparing to show Kobe, Lora was nice to let me do long sits and downs with the Open class since that's the area of Kobe's greatest training weakness. Normally in the Open class, the handlers go out of sight during this exercise. I stayed because technically Kobe was still in Novice and I didn't want Lora to have to correct my dog.

One night during the long downs Kobe happened to be lying next to a Golden Retriever who responded to a noise from another part of the building and got up. So Lora very sweetly and gently took the retriever back into line, told him to lie down, and stayed with the dog to calm him. The whole time I was watching Kobe who was watching Lora who had her back to him maybe a foot or two away. Lora continued to pet and care for the retriever. After a minute or two, the look on Kobe's face was, "That's it, I can't take it anymore. Why aren't I getting any love over here?" With that, he got up, moved straight to Lora, and pushed his nose under her arm, clearly jealous of all the attention this other dog was getting. And Kobe is quick! It took some concerted effort to unobtrusively and diplomatically move Kobe back into his correct position. If I'm going to stay a step ahead of this dog, I'd better be on my toes.

I have been introducing Kobe to retrieving so that he will be ready for the Open class. Kobe clearly understands the concept, but what he didn't seem to understand is that when I throw the dumbbell, he is supposed to return with the dumbbell, the same item I threw. We often practice at the park or at the field behind the local high school, and so far when I've thrown the dumbbell, he has come back with an empty Coke can, a softball, a candy wrapper, pinecones, a kid's sock, and once he even came back with a baseball mitt he found. If it's out there, he'll find it. Someday he'll be a great tracker. We've gone back to basics and, using a different approach, I know before long he'll be a great retriever. In the meantime, we're having fun.

Erick really enjoys his time with Kobe, and every weekend, schedule and weather permitting, takes Kobe for a long walk and some play time with his buddy Koa, a very cool boxer. The particular park where they go is undeveloped land with streams, trees, brush, and is apparently a fun haven for lizards and field mice. I have seen Kobe take off chasing lizards and other critters such as squirrels with much enthusiasm, but Erick said that at this park, Kobe is remarkable in his efforts. Erick said he's seen a video about the way that foxes hunt for small game in the snow. The fox will leap up in the air and then dive down into the snow much in the way divers slice their way through the water, the higher they go the deeper they can penetrate through the crust of snow. The call of the wild is strong, and Kobe often does the same thing. Once he spots his prey (preferably the lizards), he is a relentless hunter, often bounding off through the tall brush and leaping high into the air and diving into a big bush or a hole in the ground to catch his prey. And catch them he sometimes does! Unfortunately, on some of these occasions Kobe has also disturbed a hornet's nest, and he and Erick have had to make a hasty, tactical retreat or suffer the painful consequences.

I've been studying music for several years. Earlier this year I was preparing my music selections for the spring recital. One of my selections was a piano solo of Brahms Hungarian Dance #5. For the level at which I am able to play, this piece in its original form is a crazy hard piece to learn. I had therefore decided to be gracious to my husband's ears as well as my own and learned to play and practice it on my keyboard which allowed me to turn the volume down low so we didn't have to listen to my mistakes at such a high decibel. I'd eventually learned it well enough that I decided the time had come to practice on my piano instead of playing only on my keyboard.

With great joy one afternoon I sat down to the piano in our living room and with great exuberance began to play. Not more than three or four measures into it, my beloved Kobe began to howl for all he was worth. I immediately assumed that he must be hearing a siren far off which is the only time I had ever heard him howl. I went to him and comforted him and when he had quieted down, I went back to the piano. This time I didn't even get into the third measure before Kobe was howling with just as much gusto as I was playing. So I stopped, not yet willing to believe that there truly was a connection. However, a few more trials were enough to convince me that either Kobe loved this music and wanted nothing more than to accompany me, or maybe I'd better return to the keyboard because my playing was too painful for him to listen to. Even though there was no one else around, I felt really embarrassed at first but then I saw the whole situation as just really funny! Kobe is quite the character, and you've just got to love him. I did tell him he was not invited to the recital!

Kobe really enjoys his daily walks and runs and his play dates with his friends, but his favorite activity is tug of war. Besides having fun, this activity also provides an opportunity to fine tune other skills while improving his attention span and being great preparation for Schutzund training. While he still behaves like a puppy, at times even during training, when he's playing tug of war he gets "in the zone" to quote a popular athletic training term. Kobe is definitely prey driven, and while he does remain aware of what's going on around him, he is totally focused on his chance to get the tug toy. So we practice his "down stay" for instance until we release him to go for the toy. At those times, he works like an adult. In our Show Novice class, the instructors will often have us do the recall exercise once straight through without purposeful distractions, but the second time through the instructor may attempt to distract the dog with various toys as he's running to the handler. As previously mentioned, Kobe has a special affinity for toys that squeak, the more squeak the better. He has therefore been known to divert his attention from his recall to whatever squeaky toy has been offered. He thinks this is great fun!

One night at class, Lora's assistant, Dave, was overseeing Kobe's recall exercise. At that time, though Dave had obviously seen Kobe in class and was familiar with Kobe's fun-loving nature, he didn't personally know him very well. When it was our turn, I told Kobe to come and he came running to me with great exuberance to a nice straight sit in front of me. What a good boy! The second time through, Dave again had me call Kobe and Kobe started off very well but then instead of a squeaky toy, Dave tossed toward Kobe a tug toy and then drew it right back all in one quick motion. In a split instant, Kobe turned on a dime and ran full out "in the zone" straight for Dave. Dave handled himself very well and didn't move away, but his face turned sheet white as he watched this ninety pound Doberman barreling towards him. I knew Kobe was only interested in biting the toy but it occurred to me that if Dave was unprepared, Kobe might unintentionally knock him over so I yelled, "Kobe NO!" Bless his heart, Kobe stopped on a dime and looked at me like, "What did I do?" And Dave, the great sport and professional that he is, just laughed and said, "No problem," as his color slowly returned. (After class, I made sure to take Kobe over to Dave so Kobe could give him love, and I explained to Dave about Kobe's prey drive and his intensity in games of tug of war. It was duly noted.)

Next to God and Erick, Kobe is my best friend, constant companion, and my partner in mischief. He loves not only us but my children and grandchildren. Last Christmas, my sister-in-law, Val, was telling my then three-year-old granddaughter, Paige, the story of Little Red Riding Hood or rather little pink riding hood, as Paige was sporting a pink cape that day. Paige likes to get into stories and will sometimes act out her part. When they got to the part of the big bad wolf, I heard Paige exclaim, "Kobe can play the big bad wolf!" As the story ended, Paige was still in her role, and my sweet Kobe very patiently let Paige push him around so she could show to anyone paying attention the big bad wolf's teeth while pretending the wolf was getting ready to eat her. Kobe, who stood eye to eye with her, came up close and personal, and gave her a big lick across her beautiful little face. Reacting to her big bad wolf's approach, instead of "Oh no!" Paige came out with, "Oh gross!" New ending for the story.

Kobe waiting to play the Big Bad Wolf

Kobe has inherited some of his character from his Great Uncle Rowdy. I've been taking Kobe to Run-through classes which are designed to prepare a dog for a show ring experience. At these classes I made some new friends, one of whom I learned was very afraid of Dobermans after witnessing a Doberman attack a little girl many years before. She approached me one day after watching Kobe work. She saw Kobe's behavior both in and out of the ring and asked me with some trepidation if she might approach him. I let her know that it would be fine and she cautiously made her way over. She let Kobe smell her and within a few minutes, she and Kobe became friends. The next time they saw each other a couple of weeks later, there was no more fear or trepidation. As this lady was petting Kobe, he leaned into her, reassuring her of their friendship and melting her heart toward Dobermans in the process. Kobe is carrying on Rowdy's legacy as Mr. Congeniality.

Kobe is now two and a half years old and is starting to really come into his own. His puppyish characteristics are starting to fade away, and he's becoming an adult reflecting the quality and heritage from Rocky and Jack and the other wonderful Dobermans before him. More than anything, he is a much-loved part of our family, and the best of our adventures with him are yet to come.

I was working Kobe recently and a police officer pulled into the area where we were and asked about him. I had just put Kobe back in the car but asked the officer if he would like to meet him. He absolutely did, so I let Kobe out and introduced him. After watching me work Kobe for a few minutes and also watching Kobe take off with great exuberance after a squirrel, he remarked what a nice dog Kobe was. After telling the officer that my dog's name was Kobe, I couldn't resist sharing the story of when I had Kobe at the vet's office when he was eleven weeks old. I told how the husband of the couple I met there remarked that because of the way Kobe

Photo by Brit Rush Photography

was hiding and peering out from between my ankles, he didn't much look like "the black mamba." When I asked the officer if he thought Kobe looked like "the black mamba" yet, his answer was, "Yes, he does. No question about it."

Chapter 8

Kayla

Renaissance Gelts White Queen

M y son, Michael, grew up in our home with dogs and always had a loving relationship with them. So it came as no surprise when Michael as an adult moved into his own home that he would want a dog. Michael researched different breeds of dogs and their qualities before he

decided to get a Vizsla. When Michael was in college, the family of one of the students that he tutored, had a Vizsla, which gave Michael the desire to take a closer look at them when it was his turn to choose a puppy. Vizslas are medi-um-sized, short-haired dogs, generally high energy and won-derful companions. Of course being the good Hungarian girl that I am, I was delighted when

Michael chose a Hungarian hunting dog to become the newest member of our family.

When Kayla first arrived home to Michael from the breeder, she looked a little bewildered as most puppies would be, but it didn't take her long at all to know how much she was loved and cared for. Michael appreciates Kayla's affectionate nature, high energy, and the way she is always in tune to where Michael is. Michael was told by the breeder that Vizslas are sometimes referred to as "velcro dogs" because of their innate desire to be wherever their owner is. While this is an enviable characteristic in a dog, it can also be annoying. I would often take care of Kayla when she was a young puppy while Michael was at work. I had a home office and did not own a dog at the time, so I treasured my time with Kayla and her sweet, loving disposition. But I also found myself tripping over "Miss Velcro" with great regularity as I was helping clients and answering their questions. I also found it difficult to use the restroom without Kayla insisting that she needed to come in with me. Explaining to her that I didn't need her help was of no avail. But she learned most things quickly and continues to bring great joy to all of us.

Kayla was barely a year old when I brought Kobe home. A couple of weeks later, Michael brought Kayla over to introduce her to Kobe. Kayla thought this was a great thing. She had this little nine-week-old puppy to play with who was full of energy like her but was small enough to boss around. We were all amused to see Kayla body slam Kobe in play, and Kobe would just bounce right back up for more. She never hurt him in any way, she just seemed to have great fun being in charge of what they were playing and when. In hindsight, I probably should have tried to explain to Kayla that Kobe was a Doberman and that he would not always remain that small or be so easily pushed around. In fact, I'm sure it never occurred to Kayla that it might not be wise to teach a Doberman the art of body slamming as one day soon she might be on the receiving end of it.

Just by virtue of the amount of time they spent together, Kayla and Kobe taught each other the most interesting things. Watching his "older sister," as Kobe thought of Kayla, he learned to point. When he was a younger puppy, Kobe could rock back similarly to Kayla, lift his paw and point. Now that Kobe's closing in on ninety pounds, he's lost some of that rocking back ability but will still often point, especially when he has a big squirrel in his sights and right before he takes off in hot pursuit of his quarry. Part of a dog's training includes "honoring the point." When game is detected, a dog freezes, either pointing or crouching. If other dogs are present, they also freeze, "honoring" the first dog's point. The pointing dog remains motionless until the hunters are in position, awaiting the handler's next command.

"Honoring the point"

Since Kayla was older, I didn't think Kobe would influence her, until one day as I was watching both dogs in my backyard, I saw Kayla try to lift her leg to pee. I about fell out of my lawn chair laughing, but after trial and error, Kayla realized that this skill was clearly not for her.

One of Kayla's favorite things to do was run, and it seemed to me that from the time she was young, she could absolutely fly! Kobe as a young puppy would be half a field behind her, woofing nonstop as if to say, "Wait for me!!" But did she wait? Nooo, and just about the time she stopped to smell the roses, so to speak, and Kobe caught up to her, she would take off again. Kobe would resume his chase without much success at the time, but Kayla and Kobe running together paid off in wonderful dividends. Kobe grew up in exceptionally good condition. People would ask me how I trained and worked my dog to get him in that kind of shape, and I simply and truthfully replied, "He runs with a Vizsla." And he enjoyed every minute of it! As Kobe grew bigger, there were times I think Kayla would wonder what happened to that cute little dog she enjoyed playing with and where did this big black dog come from? Especially if they hadn't seen each other in a while. And just so you know, Kobe is two and a half years old now and can catch Miss Kayla so that they can fly together.

One of the things we all appreciate about Kayla is how smart she is and how tender and sensitive she can be. Michael told me about a time he was home sick with 102-degree fever, and instead of Kayla being her usual rambunctious self, she snuggled and cuddled with Michael as if to say, "I understand." Kayla, like many Vizslas, has a myriad of vocalizations with which to communicate, and Kayla is definitely a talker, but seeming to understand how ill Michael was, she just quietly laid near him.

Besides being smart, she can also be a conniving little sneak. Kayla, like many dogs, has unique ways to communicate her different needs; such as when she is hungry or hurt or needs to go outside. One day Kayla gave Michael her best "Daddy, play with me" woof. Whether Michael felt like it or not, he got up from his favorite Lazy Boy type chair to play with her. The minute he did, Miss Kayla promptly jumped into said chair and curled up for a nice nap. Feeling a little perturbed at having been tricked out of his chair, Michael sweetly removed Kayla from the chair and let her know that he was wise to her tricks now and reminded her that while she was a very smart girl, he was smarter.

Kayla can be so funny with some of her idiosyncrasies. For a dog that's high energy, I have seen Kayla sit almost motionless and stare at a tree if she thinks there might be a squirrel coming back to it anytime soon. And she doesn't give up. It's probably one of the qualities of a good hunting dog but when she's in the yard staring at seemingly nothing, it's funny. In addition, Kayla is often so alert (again the mark of a good dog) and can be so attentive one minute and the next she can't seem to focus on what's right in front of her.

Kayla beckoning squirrel

One time she was at my house and Kayla was napping at one of her favorite spots, the top of the back of my couch by the living room window. There is a tree and a fence probably not more than five feet from this window and from where Kayla was. I glanced over and there was a big fat squirrel just sitting on the fence probably not more than five feet from her. I said, "Kayla, squirrel!" And Kayla, knowing that I don't tease her in this manner, was wildly looking everywhere for the squirrel except at where it was. I actually took hold of her head gently with two hands and pointed her face directly at the squirrel. Again, "Kayla, squirrel!" You think she saw it? Nope. But she saw everything else that moved within one hundred feet in any direction. The squirrel hadn't moved. Maybe movement is the key.

I am glad that Kayla feels very much at home at my house. Kobe and Kayla enjoy running the Indianapolis 500 up the stairs, down the stairs, around the kitchen table, back up the stairs and into the master bedroom (if I have forgotten to close the door), up on the bed, a couple of laps around the bed, including under and through all the pillows, and back out and down the stairs. But I think Kayla's favorite thing to do is to sit up on top of the rock that is above the waterfall my husband built overlooking our mini swimming pool and survey her kingdom. She can see everything from there, including who's coming and going from our house, and anything and everything that may wish to enter the yard, with a special lookout for those infamous squirrels. That rock is situated under a tree that is ripe for squirrel activity so she can patiently sit there in shady comfort while awaiting her opportunity to pounce on the first squirrel who dares to invade Miss Kayla's personal space. Little Miss Drama Queen!

I personally think Vizslas are somehow related to hummingbirds. I've never before seen a dog whose tail can wag faster than the speed of sound. It's especially funny when Michael will make pigeon sounds against her fur and Kayla's body will be absolutely still, but the speed of her tail wag would be the envy of the best drummers around. Sometimes our dogs are more entertaining than television.

Last fall, we went to Sterling Lake in the Sierras for a long weekend. Michael of course brought Kayla, and Erick and I brought Kobe. The weekend was one long adventure. We hiked, swam, kayaked, and the dogs did everything right along with us. And when we were resting, reading, or cooking, Kayla and Kobe chased squirrels, chipmunks, birds; they missed nothing. And of course Kayla chose her personal lookout spot to hang out at times throughout the day from where she could once again see everything and make absolutely sure nothing was missed. At night in the Sierras, the temperature often drops into the 30s, even during the summer and fall. So Miss Kayla decided that the best way to stay warm was to burrow down into Michael's sleeping bag and I mean all the way to the bottom. I couldn't help but wonder where Michael put his feet with a forty-five pound Vizsla at the bottom of his sleeping bag or how he slept listening to her snore. Suffice it to say that for Christmas, Erick and I gifted Kayla with her own sleeping bag.

Besides being a loving companion and friend, Kayla is a wonderful gatekeeper. Her loyalty supersedes any other positive associations or connections. She will faithfully alert with low growling and/or barking if there is an unknown someone approaching their home, but she will always choose to be a personal protector over protecting property. From the time she was young, I saw her consistently put herself between Michael and anyone else approaching Michael's personal space. I was honestly amazed at times how grown up she could act while still so young.

Kayla's lookout

For all of Kayla's qualities that I have already shared and for so much more, I feel blessed that Kayla is part of our family. Every time I see her, Kayla makes me feel so loved. She runs to me with complete abandon, her whole body wagging almost as fast as her tail, and for a moment I experience absolute unconditional love. Moments like that make life worthwhile.

Chapter 9

Phoenix Rising

GCH Kiralyi Jen's Penny Tribute to Tucker

Those of us who spend a lot of time around and with dogs meet some wonderful and excellent dogs in a variety of breeds. And then, every now and again, you encounter one so unique that they remain unforgettable in your memory. Phoenix is such a dog. The first time I met him, Phoenix was two years old. This would have been about three years ago when my son, Michael, and I had been invited to visit Nancy Guarascio, a well-known and reputable Vizsla breeder. It was a lovely fall morning, and Michael was interested in seeing some Vizslas as he was hoping to soon get a Vizsla puppy. This of course was before Kayla became a member of our family.

We agreed to meet over at an elementary school field where Nancy often goes to run her dogs. I watched her play ball with them and noticed the excellent control she had over a number of dogs simultaneously and was impressed. If you remember from Kayla's story how Vizslas can run like the wind, it's easy to understand that overseeing a number of them at the same time could be a challenge. But Nancy's loving care and protection of her dogs was unquestionable.

Afterwards, Nancy invited us to her house. Even though we all entered the house together, Phoenix, as well as some of the other dogs, in chorus let Michael and I know that now we were on their home turf and that they would have absolutely no problem defending it. It was all very appropriate. They saw that Nancy welcomed us, and the dogs settled down.

Phoenix at the beach

We sat down, and no sooner had I found a comfortable spot on the couch, but Phoenix made himself at home next to me, put his head in my lap as if to say, "You have the privilege of petting me now." That behavior caught me unaware. I had expected that the dogs might be more cautious since we had never met before. Not Phoenix. He was in my lap and in my face, so to speak, and ready to be loved. Clearly this dog was self-assured, very outgoing, and had a sense of humor. He also figured out very quickly that I am a person who likes dogs, and he could wrap me around his paw. He also didn't take no for an answer. If I wasn't petting him to his satisfaction, he would turn on his side (still in my lap) and paw the air as if to say, "I didn't say you could stop, and the petting feels really good so please feel free to continue." Of course, I didn't mind at all. The surprises were just beginning.

As Michael and Nancy were talking, Nancy got up and turned on the television and turned the channel to an animal program that included dogs. The minute she did, Phoenix jumped off the couch and positioned himself a couple of feet in front of the television and in a most animated fashion followed the story. I watched with great amusement as his head turned left to right, back and forth following the action, adding in his "woof" at the appropriate times. I asked Nancy if all her dogs were like this. She said, "No," but in the years she's had Vizslas, she has found a number of them to be "gifted" in various ways.

Phoenix's father, Tucker (CH Jen Penny Tucker's Treasure), for example, learned by the time he was five weeks old how to climb out of the whelping box and climb onto the back of the couch where Nancy would find him with his front feet crossed as he was surveying his kingdom, which in this case was his brothers and sisters still in the box. By the time he was seven weeks old, he could climb out of the xpen, a little, enclosed, portable gated area, onto the kitchen counter and jump off onto the floor. Right there, that would have told me I'd better keep my eye on this puppy and be ready to not be surprised by anything he did. When Tucker was ten weeks old, Nancy took him to the vet after he was stung by a bee. The vet removed the stinger but decided to keep Tucker for a little while just to keep his eye on him. A few hours later, Nancy called to see how Tucker was doing. When the phone was answered, she could hear howling in the background and asked, "Is that Tucker in the background?" The reply was, "Yes, and please come get him, he's driving us nuts!" Tucker was obviously a dog who could make his presence known.

Tucker turned out to be a great show dog and not always when he was actually being shown in the ring. At one particular show, Tucker had come with his handler. She had just let Tucker out of the Utility Vehicle and was getting ready to put his show lead on to go into the show ring, when he bolted and took off. It's like he was saying, "I know my mom is here and I'm going to find her!" Nancy was inside watching another class finishing up and waiting for Tucker's turn in the ring. As Nancy was enjoying herself at ring side, she heard, "Loose dog!" "It's a Vizsla!" And while most everyone was likely watching, there came Tucker leaping from ring to ring until he saw Nancy and then took a flying leap into her arms. I asked Nancy if anyone got a picture of Tucker leaping from ring to ring (it would have been great for this story) and she said, "No, only in my mind. But it was a hallmark moment!"

Tucker—Photo by Cook Photography

Being gifted seems to run in Phoenix's family. His aunt Lucy (CH Jen's Penny Lucky Lucy CD), is a counter surfer. In other words, don't leave anything on the counter if you leave the room, because if it looks good, smells good, or likely tastes good, it will be gone before you get back. When Lucy was ten years old, Nancy took Lucy to her sister Cheri's house for the Christmas holidays. They were preparing breakfast, and in the kitchen was two pounds of bacon draining on paper towels over a plate on the counter. While everyone else was otherwise occupied, Cheri left the kitchen for no more than two or three minutes. When she returned, she realized the bacon was missing and asked, "Hey Nancy, what did you do with the bacon?" Nancy replied that she hadn't done anything with the bacon, and when they looked down, there were the paper towels on the floor with the plate licked clean. "Lucy, you have some explaining to do!" Cheri exclaimed. Lucy, looking totally guilty but equally unrepentant, licked her lips as if to say, "Delicious!"

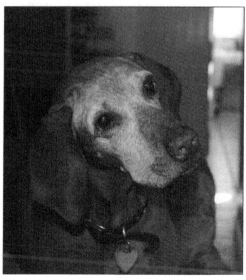

Counter Surfer Lucy

Do you think Lucy had learned anything from this experience? Nope. Lucy has been known to ingest an entire stick of butter, and on one occasion she swiped a whole loaf of pumpkin bread that had been packaged as a gift. Lucy, like the lady she is, untied the bow and laid out the cellophane that the bread had been wrapped in and left it on the floor absolutely licked clean . . . again. Lucy is now fourteen years old and just a few days prior to this writing, she struck again. Nancy's friend, Bob, was home watching Lucy and was planning on making himself a sandwich. To that end, he took a half meat loaf out of the refrigerator and set it on the counter. Big mistake. Actually, that wasn't the mistake. The mistake was that he left the room for a minute with Lucy unattended. Upon returning, he discovered that the meatloaf in its entirety was missing and Lucy was licking her lips, totally delighted and satisfied with her snack. I have a feeling there have been many other sneak attacks of the food thief. I personally have yet to see anything left out on Nancy's countertops and now I totally understand why.

Then there's Peppermint Patty (CH Jen's Penny Peppermint Patty), Phoenix's aunt and a litter sister to Tucker and Lucy. Nancy said Patty is a snob that is nicknamed "Bratty Patty." There is a reason for this. She seems to feel entitled to getting her own way and when she doesn't, there are consequences. For instance, you can tell when she's upset because she might go from room to room pulling down all the towels. Not sure what payoff she gets from this behavior, but certainly this

Peppermint Patty—Photo by Cook Photography

activity is an attention getter. Patty belongs to a distinguished judge and clearly thinks that she should live a privileged life. She's very selective about her friends, her food, and her bed. Once when she got mad at her mom (the judge), she ate a hole in mom's cashmere sweater. I wonder if she could be held in contempt? But Miss Patty can also shine. When she's in the show ring, she knows it. Her handler can have the bait in one hand and Patty's tail gently held up to show her elegance with her other hand and Patty can hold that pose undeterred for five minutes. It's as if she's saying, "Okay, I'm here now, no need to look at anyone else." Of course, if the handler isn't careful, Patty can also steal the bait and include the handler's fingers in the bite. It's a hint to the handler to not take her eyes off Patty.

Patty Best Opposite Sex—Photo by Cook
Photography

Patty has had some exceptional offspring. Baci (GOLD Grand CH Jen's Penny Matra Baci's Boogie Fever) is Patty's grandson. Baci is pronounced Bachi and in Italian is the word for "kiss." When Nancy told me about Baci, and since Vizslas are Hungarian dogs, I at first assumed she spelled it Bacsi, which is the Hungarian word for "uncle," but is often used as a title to address a gentleman as a sign of respect. Baci lived up to both translations of the name. He is a licker and is also a gentleman. Nancy described Baci as the "coolest dog." He has a rock solid temperament, and he seems to know instinctively how to conduct himself in any given situation. That's a rare quality indeed.

Diving Baci

In 2011, Baci won at Eukanuba, a very prestigious dog show that was held in Florida that year. He won Best of Breed over sixty-six other Vizsla champions in attendance under a Hungarian judge. In fact, Baci was the number three Vizsla in the country that year. On their way back to California after the show, the pilot of the airplane was so taken with Baci (Baci is also a service dog and therefore was permitted in the cabin), he invited him into the cockpit where he wanted his picture taken with the dog so he could show Baci to his wife. When they finally landed, the pilot and crew didn't allow any of the passengers to disembark until they all had a chance to give Baci kisses and say good-bye. That's charisma. I have got to meet this dog! A note of interest: Baci is a half-brother to Kayla. Their father is CH Renaissance Lord of Th'Dance, call name Konner.

It is obvious to see that Phoenix comes by his gifts honestly. He is five years old now and seeing him after three years, he has blossomed into a mature, beautiful, and loving dog. I was also very pleased to see that Phoenix has not lost his sense of humor. When I came for a recent visit to complete the interview for this story, Phoenix and Lucy both met me at the door. They were both barking, but had Nancy not been there and welcomed me in telling the dogs it was okay, I do not believe there is any way I would have gotten past Phoenix. I am glad. I already admired and respected him, but I realized that under no circumstances should he be underestimated in his role as a gatekeeper. When it comes to protecting Nancy, there is no compromise. Once Phoenix saw that Nancy was at ease with me, so was he.

Then the Phoenix I love and remember emerged. He has remained his loving, playful self but has taken his television watching to another level. Nancy turned on the television to a canine cartoon program and off Phoenix went. The television screen is much higher now than it used to be and he didn't just sit and watch and bark. He added in jumping up close to the height of the television and barking, while he did acrobatic type turns. (This time I came with a camera and took pictures. A picture really is worth a thousand words, isn't it?) It's one of those things you almost have to see to really appreciate, especially the passion with which Phoenix enjoys these shows.

Phoenix is a happy dog and clearly finds ways to enjoy his life. For instance, he loves to play games. One of his favorite games is to come down the stairs ahead of the other dogs, sneak around the corner, and lie in wait for the others to come. As soon as they get close to the bottom step, Phoenix will jump out, bombarding them with barks and growls (all in play), blocking the bottom of the stairs by jumping back and forth much like a goalie blocking a soccer ball being kicked. Of course, eventually the other dogs really want to get outside and therefore they insist that Phoenix step aside,

Phoenix watching TV

which he always does. It's all in fun!

Phoenix is not all play but shows very well and is a Grand Champion. But to Nancy, he's her faithful and constant companion. I noticed that no matter how much Phoenix and I were playing, the moment Nancy got up, he was totally focused on what she was doing, and if she left the room, he went with her. He was never unaware of her presence. Another velcro dog, and I mean that with all affection!

Phoenix moving with his handler, Stephanie

I once asked Nancy what she appreciated the most about having Vizslas. She said she found them to be intelligent, regal, sweet, unusual, and at times striking in appearance. But much more than that, they are family and a lot of fun to live with. Based on the stories Nancy has told me about her dogs, I'm thinking that they probably keep her on her toes and that living with Vizslas, there's never a dull moment.

Chapter 10

Gus and Xena

AM/CAN CH Alturi's Gallant Gus CH Gold Run's
Princess Xena

I met my friend Mary Shapiro when she expressed an interest in carpooling up to Concord together for our dogs' conformation class. I wasn't sure putting Kobe, my Doberman, in a car with an unknown other dog was a good idea until she mentioned that she had a female Vizsla. Kobe, having grown up with a Vizsla, seems fully convinced that Vizslas were put on the earth by God for the purpose of being loved and protected, and I knew Kobe would be delighted. I wasn't as certain that Mary's dog, Zora, would feel the same way, but all went well. Concord was an hour drive for us each way so we had plenty of opportunity to share each other's dog stories. Mary shared the following story with me, and I thought this was a gatekeeper story for the ages.

This incident occurred some years before I met Mary. At the time she owned a Rhodesian Ridgeback named Gus and a Vizsla named Xena. Gus was a product of excellent breeding.

In fact, his father had won the breed at Westminster. Gus was calm, confident, loving, and protective. He was also excellent with kids, very smart, and sweet. And he would follow Xena around. Xena was a very well-bred Vizsla, an extrovert, smart, loved agility trials, and nothing fazed her. Here was a forty pound dog that would chase coyotes if they came near her fenced in property. Above all, Gus and Xena were family.

It was during the day in the spring of the year, and Mary's husband was at work. It was a nice day, and Mary was in the kitchen taking the meat off the bones of a stewed chicken that she intended to use for making soup. The dogs were of course right next to her hoping for yummy scraps as snacks when they clearly alerted to someone's presence and left Mary's side, barking and growling for all they were worth. Mary turned to face an intruder who had likely come in through the garage to the family room/ kitchen combo where Mary was. There stood a man about forty to forty-five years old, with short dark hair, about 5 foot 10 inches, clean cut, clean clothes, but totally unfamiliar to Mary. She asked him, "Who are you? What are you doing here? What do you want?" I guess with the two dogs right in front of him barking and growling the intruder did not appear to be available for a chat, nor did it seem like the right time for one. Moreover, Gus kept jumping up and bumping the intruder, who appeared to be unarmed and was busily shielding his body with his forearm.

The intruder was between Mary's house phone and Mary, so she decided to go to the neighbor's house to call the police. The dogs seemed to have everything well in hand with Xena barking like crazy and Gus continuing his tirade, with having added bumping the guy's head with his nose. It's important to note here that neither dog had bitten the intruder but were definitely and assertively holding him at bay. So Mary ran out the back door and covered the quarter of a mile to her neighbor's house as fast as she could. When her neighbor saw her, she became alarmed and called 911. A police car arrived in about six to seven minutes, and they waited another five to ten minutes for two units from the sheriff's department to arrive since Mary lived within their jurisdiction.

The dispatcher from the sheriff's department kept Mary on the phone until the units arrived. Before the dispatcher ended the call, she came on the line and asked Mary if she knew someone named Mark. Mary said, "No, why?" "Because someone named Mark just called 911 from your house requesting help." He wouldn't say why but the cause would soon become apparent. Mary met the officers out in front of her house where she clarified for them where all the doors to the outside were and where the intruder was. All this time the dogs were still barking. As the officers were ready to go in, Mary said to them, "Please don't hurt my dogs!" One of the officers asked Mary what the dogs' names were. "Gus and Xena," she replied. The sheriff deputies went in and without incident sent the dogs out to Mary. The deputies arrested Mark and removed him from the premises.

Before the officers left, they asked Mary to check to see if anything was missing and the only thing that was gone were the chicken skins that Mark had apparently tried to bribe Gus and Xena with in an attempt to bargain with them for his release. But Gus and Xena's love, loyalty, and protection of their mom were non-negotiable. I'm certain that Gus and Xena were hailed for some time to come, not only by family and friends but also by the sheriff's department deputies who were able to easily apprehend an intruder with the help of two loving and courageous dogs. I'm also certain this story was often re-told by the officers as one of those rare events when an intruder called 911 for help to be rescued from two dogs, each with a "never give up" attitude.

Some years later, Mary had three Vizslas, one whose name was Chance. Chance was a four- or five-year-old, seventy-five pound male, which is very large for a Vizsla. But he was a loving dog who slept with Mary's thirteen-year-old daughter and was gentle and wonderful with both her daughters. Chance was also good with other dogs, did not have an aggressive personality, and was a great and trustworthy addition to their family.

One day, two of her dogs were in the house asleep on the couch when Mary went outside to dig up weeds in her front pasture. Chance accompanied her and had remained out there with her when four guys drove up to her, driving a newer, clean, white sedan. Since Mary lives on three acres of land, these people were not "just driving by" so to speak.

They stopped the car, and Mary asked them what they wanted. Though the visual evidence suggested otherwise, they claimed to be workmen looking for work. Mary said she didn't need any help and asked them to leave. They continued their approach and Mary, being alone, knew that this was not a good situation. She positioned herself at the driver's door with Chance by her side. Addressing the driver and repeating that there was no work available, she once again asked them to leave. But they would not. As the driver began to open his door, Mary firmly told him, "You get out of that car and before you take one step, this dog will rip your throat out before you can lay a hand on me." Mary knew instinctively that the man would then look at the dog sitting quietly but alertly next to her and assess the potential validity of her claim. Mary also knew that Chance did not like men because he had been abused by men as a puppy before he came to live with her. The minute the driver made eye contact with him, Chance immediately began barking and growling, clearly making a believer out of him, though Chance had taken no further action. The driver, then re-thinking the wisdom of his intent, wisely and slowly pulled his leg back into the car and left.

We always hope and pray that our dogs will never be in a situation where their help is needed to defend us, and that's not why most of us have them. But we're very grateful for the times when these gatekeepers become a deterrent to a bad situation potentially becoming worse.

Chapter 11

Joie

DC Freedom's Pride of Northstar SC, RE, CDX, AX, AXJ,
HIC, CGC, FCH, VCX

I have recognized Rhodesian Ridgebacks for many years
because of the ridge along their back that is unmistakably unique. But my first real interest in them was stirred
when I heard the story of Gus and Xena and their remarkable
ability to keep an intruder at bay. I noticed that there were
a number of Ridgebacks training at the same facility where
I train Kobe, and week after week I noticed how nice the
dogs were and what an excellent rapport one of the owners
especially had with them. That's how I met Carol Vesely.

When I went to visit Carol and her husband Jerry, I knew
that they had had Rhodesian Ridgebacks for twenty-five
years. I didn't know what to expect in regards to the dogs at
all. I was invited in and found myself greeted by a number
of dogs, one of which in particular made it clear that I was
a stranger and that she would be watching me. That was
Joie and I liked her immediately. What I liked first was
that she looked straight at me as she was barking out her

message. She never turned her back, or ran around me in order to intimidate but took her stand without any unnecessary theatrics. I respected her for that. As soon as she saw that I was welcome and expected, she settled down, although at least for the first hour I was there every time I glanced at her, she was still watching me. Good girl. The dogs were not overly friendly at first, which I learned is typical of the breed, but I found their demeanor refreshing as they settled down quickly regardless of my presence.

Joie

I had done a little preliminary research online on Ridgebacks before coming to the interview for this story. I read that Ridgebacks are loyal, intelligent, strong-willed, and that they have a "penchant for mischief." (I thought Kobe would be great friends with these dogs.) As Carol began to share about her dogs, I learned that Ridgebacks are sight and scent hounds that don't have a great work ethic unless it's something that they really want to do.

I also learned some things I had never heard of and, looking at the dogs, couldn't even imagine. For instance, Rhodesian Ridgebacks were originally from Southern Africa where they were bred and trained to protect ranchers from the large game in Africa, the lion in particular, which they could keep at bay while awaiting their master to make the kill. The dogs would go out as a pack and surround the lion and, taking turns, they would dart in toward the lion and quickly retreat as to keep the lion off guard. (This is when I understood Gus's jumping up and bumping the intruder; this is inbred behavior). These dogs are incredibly fast and they would have to be to keep from being mauled by the lion. They are out there with no handler but have learned to think for themselves and make their own decisions.

They are incredibly smart but in a different way than most of us are accustomed to seeing. Most working dogs we normally see respond to the commands of the trainer teaching them what to do and how to do it in any given situation. Ridgebacks prefer to figure it out for themselves. That's not at all to say that they can't be taught by a handler, but rather that these dogs process the information they are given differently as if to think through the solution till it makes sense to them.

As I sat in Carol's dining room and looked at the dogs laying around on the various comfy dog beds sleepily yawning at us, I had a hard time imagining them holding a lion or anything else at bay. They hardly got up while I was there unless it was time to go out and play a little, and when I had watched them at the training facility, they honestly looked bored a good deal of the time. Carol explained that what I'd seen was just one side of their nature.

She and her husband take the dogs to what she called "lure coursing" events (I had no idea what that was). Apparently there is a course set up with lures (white kitchen trash bags sliced up, which when they move, resemble rabbits), and these lures are moved by a set of pulleys at various speeds depending on the speed of the dogs on any particular heat. The dogs are evaluated on their ability to follow the lures around the entire course. The dogs are judged on five categories: their enthusiasm, speed, agility, endurance, and how closely they follow the course. I asked Carol if I might accompany them to such an event so I could see this for myself. All I was seeing at the moment were dogs enjoying a lazy afternoon, not motivated to get up and do much moving around at all. Carol did say that most of the time her dogs are "couch potatoes." That certainly rang true.

The day came when I had the opportunity to accompany Carol, Jerry, and a couple of their friends with their dogs to a lure coursing trial. Was I ever in for a surprise! These sweet-tempered, gentle couch potatoes turn into crazy (in the best possible way) prey-driven, manic dogs when it was their turn to run the course. To my amazement, it took two able bodied, healthy, trained handlers to be able to control just one dog from his/her crate to the starting line.

(Please see the pictures included; they speak for themselves.) Carol said that these dogs are not normally vocal, but I found out that when they are at the starting line, whatever they have held in comes out in abundance as they're waiting their turn to begin the hunt.

Joie at the starting line

When they were released to run the course, these dogs were a sight to behold. At times, I could barely see their feet touching the ground and their intensity was visible in every fiber of their being. (See Joie's picture.) It was awe inspiring. All that I had heard and read about the origins of this breed being able to think for themselves, problem solve, and hold lions at bay came to life before my eyes in light of their speed, power, and ability to adapt to the course.

Joie—Photo by Kim Souza

At the end of the course, they have the opportunity to at least briefly enjoy catching their prey. Some dogs, like Joie, were not really interested in surrendering the prey that they had caught, and as I watched Carol and Jerry try to regain control of her, I understood how much training, strength, patience, and endurance it takes to properly care for these dogs. In the entire process from start to finish, I saw the commitment and love that Carol and Jerry have for their dogs and the trust that they have inspired in them. Carol said that one of the most consistent behaviors in their Ridgebacks is that the dogs always want to be with them. That day, that bond was so evident, and I could see why.

Like most dogs, Ridgebacks have their peculiarities. Apparently Carol's dogs don't like water, don't want to run through sprinklers, and don't want to be out in the rain unless of course they have caught sight of prey in their vicinity. At those times, nothing else matters. Of course, that's why Jerry and Carol don't generally let their dogs off leash when they go for walks. Ridgebacks want to be with you except when they find prey. They are so prey driven that they'll take off after their quarry, and it's most improbable that you'll get them back until they've either caught or lost their prey. I can see how protecting Ridgebacks can be a challenge, but Carol and Jerry clearly rise to that challenge and do anything and everything to ensure the safety and well-being of their dogs.

Prey isn't however the only thing that motivates the dogs. Some months ago, they were all out enjoying a walk when a gentleman named Marty met them on their route. They stopped to chat for a few minutes and all was well until Marty, in the course of conversation, made an exaggerated movement in demonstrating how big something was. Joie, perceiving a threat, stood her ground between

Carol and Marty, making it abundantly clear that making any further exaggerated movements that close to mom and dad was ill-advised. Joie is a true gatekeeper who does the minimal necessary to get her point across in protecting her loved ones.

After all this, I was somewhat amused when Carol mentioned that there is an actual silly side to these dogs. Generally that quality tends to be more characteristic of the males than the females. Indy (FC Northstar's Let Freedom Ring SC RN TD CD AX AXJ CGC HIC VC), for instance, loves going around and taking paper towels or napkins off the table. He must think that there is either something characteristically interesting or fun about them or perhaps hopes that everyone will enjoy his comedic performance and he'll get a treat out of the deal. These dogs seem to always be thinking ahead. One thing Kobe and Indy have in common is their love for barking at brooms or vacuums in use. And it's not the kind of barking that indicates their fear or protective instincts but rather the common "woofing" that's just pure fun!

Ridgebacks apparently also love to jump. They are large, powerful dogs, but it still amazed me when Carol told me that one of her other dogs, Aja, jumped a four-foot gate because she didn't want to be confined to the kitchen area anymore—when she was pregnant! Apparently, all it takes is the right motivation and these dogs can do most anything once they've set their minds to it. And it seems that that's the key.

It appears to me by what I've witnessed and experienced, that outside of the show dog world, Ridgebacks are relatively unknown much beyond their size and appearance. I'm hoping that this story will help to change that. This is a breed that carries an amazing history and great character. Knowing them is a unique experience that I am convinced many would enjoy greatly if they would only take the opportunity to do so.

Chapter 12

Lulu

Charms Clair de Luna CGC, TDI

Toward the end of the summer of 2012, I had decided it was time to fine-tune Kobe's obedience training so I signed him up for the Advanced Novice class with Santa Clara Dog Training Club. Kobe was a little over a year old and was a big puppy full of typical puppy antics. It was in this class that I met my friend Mary Schreiner and her dog Lulu.

Lulu is a silver standard poodle who was two years old at the time. My prior exposure to poodles had been limited, and most of the ones I had met tended to be somewhat high strung. So I made an effort to reign in my naturally exuberant Doberman puppy primarily because we were in an obedience class but also to not stress out any of the other dogs in the class, especially dogs like Lulu who I had assumed might be easily frightened.

One evening as we were working on our recall exercise, my efforts were put to the test. The recall exercise entails me, the handler, leaving my dog on a sit/stay command, crossing to the other side of the ring, turning to face my dog, and then calling him. In theory, my dog should then come and sit directly in front of me, fully expecting lots of love and praise. So when it was my turn, I left Kobe on a sit/stay command, crossed to the other side of the ring, turned to face him, and called, "Kobe, come!" Kobe, being the wonderful working dog that he is, came barreling toward me at a full run (I was so proud!). He was almost to me when at the last possible moment he detoured to position himself right in front of Lulu. Not only that, but he gave her his absolutely best and obvious invitation to play. As the class was trying hard to stop laughing, I took hold of Kobe's collar and repositioned him in front of me. Throughout all this Miss Lulu (as I often find myself referring to her), remained perfectly in place, absolutely unfazed by Kobe's unexpected approach. Right then, I realized that some, if not many, of my preconceptions of at least some poodles were totally incorrect. In the weeks and months that followed, Mary and I and Lulu and Kobe became friends.

Mary and her husband, Bob, actually got Lulu as a puppy when they had been married a little more than a year. Bob had insisted that the puppy they get be a poodle. Lulu left an immediate impression by trying to nibble on Mary's engagement ring. Just like a young lady, Lulu was apparently aware that diamonds were a girl's best friend. As I got to know Lulu, I was thinking that she herself was a rare find and a treasure in the world of dogs, and poodles in particular. Mary said that as Lulu was maturing, she found her to be very sweet, funny, affectionate, and smart. The longer I knew her, the more I saw that she had all of those qualities and more. For one thing, being friends with Kobe proved beyond a doubt that Lulu was also very patient and not easily rattled. She resisted his persistent invitations to play during class and showed him an example of a well-mannered, self-restrained dog. Mr. "happy-go-lucky" Kobe was learning by her example and enjoyed having a friend in class.

Mary was actually training Lulu to become a therapy dog, but sometime before Lulu became one, Mary took Lulu, who was still a puppy, to visit her father who was at an Alzheimer's and dementia care facility. When they arrived, Mary found her father actively writing, convinced that he was at work. Lovingly, Lulu put her head on his lap to comfort and show love. She didn't seem to care what he was doing, only sensing that he was in need of that tender touch. Lulu, with her solid, stable temperament, was a blessing to everyone there. Even though she was so young, she seemed to know instinctively who the residents were and who the staff members were. She was gentle and careful about giving love to the residents but felt safe to be her puppy self, having fun jumping up on the staff, obviously briefly forgetting her ladylike manners. I had the privilege of watching Lulu test for her Therapy Dog title and am convinced Lulu will bring joy and comfort to many.

Lulu is great with children to the point of never hurting them even in her own defense. Yet she is a wonderful gatekeeper. The first time I went to Mary's house, I heard Lulu bark, sounding the alarm that someone was approaching, and she definitely sounded serious. She is consistent in this behavior. Once Mary opened the door and invited me in, and Lulu looked at me in such a way as if to say, "Wait a minute, I know you! You love me and usually have treats, let's see, in your right pocket if I remember right." With that, she stuck her nose in my pocket like it was the most natural thing in the world. And yes, I did bring her treats, and she remembered exactly what I had and where she could find it. Smart and discerning dog.

Seeing Lulu in class week after week, I could tell that she was very aware of her surroundings, which is definitely one of the qualities in a good protector. Our classes at that time of year were outdoors at the local fairgrounds. One of the exercises in the Novice class is the long sits and downs.

The long sits are for a period of one minute, and the long downs are for three minutes, although the instructor at his or her discretion can vary the times so the dogs don't learn to anticipate the end of the exercise.

One night during this phase of the class, Lulu and Kobe were next to each other. It wasn't intentional but I figured sooner or later Kobe would need to learn to resist the temptation to move even if he did have a cute little girl in Lulu sitting next to him. Neither dog moved a muscle, but I noticed on the long down that Kobe alerted to something behind him. It was dark and I saw nothing abnormal, but then I noticed that Lulu was also focused on likely the same something. At first I was concerned because none of the other dogs were paying any attention to whatever it was, and I was definitely praying that Kobe and Lulu weren't planning some exciting getaway as soon as the exercise was finished. Of course Kobe would be initiating such a plan if there was one, but to their credit, neither dog moved. But no amount of encouragement to look at me thwarted Kobe's attention from whatever was there, and Lulu also remained undeterred. After class someone went to investigate and found that there was an injured fox not far behind the class ring. Our wonderful gatekeepers were at work even away from home.

That wasn't the only time Lulu was on watch. Another typical example was a time after Bob and Mary had taken Lulu hiking with them. After hiking, they stopped at a restaurant, and while Bob went for food, Mary and Lulu remained outside. As Mary sat down, she noticed a man about ten yards away talking to himself. He was not super close but close enough that Lulu remained on alert. As sweet as she looks (and she does), she's a big dog, and when she's alert, her presence is a deterrent to strangers and a comfort to family and friends.

I have seen in Lulu such a multi-faceted personality that always seems to be appropriate for the occasion. She's focused and serious when she needs to be but can also put on quite a comedic performance. Her joy and exuberance is contagious. I have seen her play with three dogs at once before class or at least try to. She can prance back and forth between dogs with utmost precision and not wear down. The energizer bunny has nothing on her. But I've never seen her out of control. When I was visiting Mary and Lulu at home, Mary had Lulu show me her dance ritual when she's having fun outside. This of course entails her prancing routine but then includes running around in small tight circles barking, her tail wagging like crazy the whole time. Talk about multi-tasking; Lulu could teach the course. More than anything, Lulu is smart, loyal, full of love, and I am better for knowing her.

Chapter 13

Casey

We have been good friends with our next door neighbors, the Mantes, ever since we moved into this neighborhood twenty-three years ago. Incidentally, these are the same neighbors that Robin visited and relieved of their chicken. And yes, we are still good friends. They know that we have Dobermans. So I was speechless when one day their daughter, Cathy Mante, came home with a Pit Bull that she named Casey. My first thought was, *I don't believe this. A ninety pound Doberman and a seventy-five pound Pit Bull will be living next door to each other. This is going to be fun* (?!).

Pit Bulls have quite a reputation and like most everyone else, I heard many of the horror stories of Pit Bulls attacking people, attacking other dogs, other animals, and causing massive damage and/or even killing them. Since Kobe is very much an alpha dog and not likely to back down from anything or anyone, I was determined that I would keep Kobe as far away from Casey as was possible. From early on Kobe and Casey barked at each other through the fence, but Kobe is never out unsupervised and the barking never seemed to escalate to other signs of aggression on either side. Most often when Casey was a puppy, I would see Mr.

Mante out walking the dog, or more accurately, Casey was walking at quite a clip and Mr. Mante was trying hard to keep up. I often wondered who was walking whom but to Mr. Mante's credit, he never gave up and Casey clearly loves him. I would also often see Casey when I was coming or going from home and finally decided to stop and meet her.

I remember the day well. Cathy and a friend of hers were out front, and I thought that that was as good a day as any for introductions. I took a deep breath and went over there. Casey saw me approaching and with all long, powerful strides came towards me. I am not afraid of dogs and can generally handle myself wisely around them, but I have to admit that seeing a Pit Bull running toward me unhindered was totally unnerving, and when she jumped on me, I briefly wondered in what condition I would survive this encounter. Fortunately for me, I had enough common sense to plant my feet solidly figuring rightly that Casey was a phenomenal force of strength to be reckoned with. And she was. I managed to remain on my feet and since Cathy was there saying it was okay for me to be there, I found myself being joyfully licked and welcomed to their yard. Since then, if she is at her gate when I come home, Casey prances around at the gate with her whole body wagging until I go over and pet her, praise her, and just give her love.

As I continue to get to know her, I find Casey to be so very different from what I expected. She is sweet-tempered, definitely energetic, very loving, and I found that a Pit Bull can even be tenderhearted because Casey is living proof.

One example of this was one day when Cathy took Casey to a dog park to play. They were already getting ready to leave when they noticed that someone was just arriving with what turned out to be a three-month-old Pit Bull puppy. The dogs were introduced and both Cathy and the owner of the puppy were amazed to see the instant rapport between the two. Casey shadowed the puppy protecting it from the other dogs. When the puppy would stop, Casey would stand over the puppy as though she was a garage that the puppy could stand in and be protected. Everyone watching thought that was the sweetest thing.

I asked Cathy why she chose a Pit Bull as an addition to their family. Cathy said she had wanted a dog for some time, had always liked the look of the Pit Bull, and wanted a dog that was short-haired, loyal, loving, active, and athletic. When she found a friend who had a litter, she went and picked out her puppy. Casey was the runt of the litter but turned out to be everything Cathy was looking for and more.

As a young puppy, Cathy took Casey to an AKC recommended puppy class. I'm sure she got pointers on how to let the family walk her instead of the reverse, as well as the usual necessary skills, like sitting, staying, and coming. She graduated with her diploma, and because she was willing to try anything and everything presented to her, without fear or hesitation, she was awarded the honor of "Most Courageous Puppy."

Casey, like most dogs, loves to run and play. In fact, she will bring you toys to play with and can be rather persistent until she gets her way. But she is not out of control and most of the time seems eager to please family and friends. This shows the good breeding in her and the love with which she is being raised. Casey, like many young ladies, also loves to sunbathe. Of course she has no reason to be concerned about sunburns or other negative impacts of too much sun. She's lovely and she knows it.

Regardless of how great a dog Casey is, I approached introducing Kobe to Casey with some serious trepidation. I knew it would be a good thing if they could get along but at the same time protecting my dog is very important to me. I'm not sure what I thought would happen, but it definitely wasn't what actually happened. Both dogs were on leash.

There were maybe a few seconds of very cautious tiptoeing around each other and then nothing else but wagging tails and the joyful yips of a new friendship. That's probably been more than a year ago now and since then there hasn't been a bark, growl, or any other negative anything toward each other. On the other hand, Kobe and Casey have excellent communication between each other. When someone approaches either one of our yards and the dogs are outside, they protect the premises together. They don't miss a thing, and the two of them together present a formidable sight. A Doberman and a Pit Bull as good friends. Truth really is sometimes stranger than fiction.

At home, Casey has a very unique relationship with each member of the family. Casey knows everyone's normal routine for each day. For instance, Casey sleeps downstairs, but at 8:00 am, she will start scratching at the door. She is an excellent family alarm clock. If there's no response, she may upgrade to woofing to make sure her job is done. Unfortunately, she isn't close enough to just reach over and turn off like an alarm clock, so at least one someone actually has to get up. But since they are greeted with nothing but love, it's a wonderful way to start the day. She looks forward to playing ball with Mr. Mante, and she knows who else will go to work at what time and when they come home. This way she can plan to have some undivided attention from everyone. She gets lots of walk time and play time every day. Mrs. Mante did tell me that if the truth be told, she is still a little wary of Casey, especially when Casey gets rambunctious. Of course as Mrs. Mante is telling me this, Cathy confided to me that whenever she thinks no one is watching, her mother will sneak little goodie tidbits down to Casey who is sitting adoringly by her side. Casey's love for the family and their love for her is clearly evident.

According to Cathy, if there are any challenges to having Casey, it's making sure that all Casey's needs are met, especially with regard to enough exercise, and also getting people, especially her mother, to warm up to her and feel comfortable with her. I totally understand this. I have a few friends who won't come over to our house because we have a Doberman. And Pit Bulls probably have a worse reputation. But Casey is a sweet-spirited, loving dog with a very stable temperament. As hesitant as I was about her when she came home to live with the Mantes, I am that much happier that she's our neighbor and loving friend.

Chapter 14

Ranger

Lorac's Texas Ranger UDX, TDX, RE, NA, NAJ, HXAS, VCD1

Australian Shepherds are some of the most fun dogs to watch work. That's my own opinion of course, but I believe many would agree with me. Back in the 1970s, I was actively showing my dogs, as well as dogs belonging to others in AKC Obedience Trials. I saw many Aussies compete and watched some of them in amazement because of the obvious joy they experienced at all levels of training. Aussies are also greatly valued for their versatility and trainability in herding sheep, cattle, and most any type of stock. When I lived in Humboldt County in Northern California, I came across a lot of working Australian Shepherds on ranches and there too I saw them to be excellent working dogs and therefore had utmost respect for them. However, I never had any particular personal interest in them one way or another. All that changed when I met Ranger.

Ranger is a blue merle male Australian Shepherd that belongs to Lora Cox, the instructor whom I introduced in Kobe's story. She would bring Ranger into class from time to time for demonstrating certain training techniques and sometimes to work certain skills along with the rest of the class. I was impressed with Ranger's precision, his excitement at the chance to work, and his obvious love for and attentiveness to Lora. But my particular affinity for Ranger developed one night as Kobe and I were watching the end of the Open class while waiting for our Show Novice class to begin.

As mentioned in an earlier chapter, the last activity in the Open class are the long sits and downs, the sits for a period of three minutes and the downs for a period of five minutes with the handlers out of sight of the dogs for each of the two exercises. In the Novice class, the sits are for one minute and the downs are for three minutes. Kobe and I were well off the sidelines of the training ring, and Ranger was doing his long sit toward the farther end of the building away from the door. He was sitting perfectly still until Lora was out of sight. If I had to venture a guess as to what may have been going on in his mind, he would have been saying, "I wonder, if I look innocent enough, if anyone would notice that I'm making my way toward where I saw my mom go?" I couldn't help but smile as I watched as Ranger tried nonchalantly to get up just far enough to slowly scoot in the direction of the door. Of course the door was on the other side of the building so I was very much interested in following his tactics. With another instructor and an assistant on the floor, Ranger's initial efforts were quickly thwarted. I don't think it occurred to Ranger that since all the dogs were sitting in a straight line, his movement might in fact be easily observed. I'm not sure that he would have cared. Nevertheless, Ranger was gently escorted back into line, told again to stay and was left.

After this happened a couple more times, Ranger went to Plan B. This time he likely figured Plan A was never going to work so he might as well without pretense just get up and go find mom. He didn't get more than a few feet before he was caught and the instructor replaced Ranger in line. As this was being done, someone else called to Lora, "Your dog keeps getting up, what do you want us to do?" Lora laughingly poked her head in the door and said, "Kill him!" Anyone who knew Lora and how much she loves her dogs and how good she is to them and with them, understood the momentary frustration that most of us feel when our dogs know very well what's expected, and they simply have a different agenda that they consider to be more important. I couldn't help but giggle as I watched.

The entire time this scenario was unfolding, Ranger hardly took his eyes off the door, especially after seeing Lora poke her head in the door, which confirmed to him exactly where she was. What happened next made me realize not only how smart Ranger is, how determined he can be when he sets his mind to something, but that his love and loyalty to Lora supersedes anything else. Ranger was obviously determined that he would accomplish his mission to get to mom. Now, as long as he knew the instructor was watching him, he sat absolutely motionless. But every time the instructor turned his attention to the other dogs, Ranger would get up just enough so that he could re-sit again in an instant. Never mind that he was out of position, he was determined to not allow anyone to catch him in the act. Not only that, but he would actually look around and then look up at the instructor as if to say, "Who me? Move? Did you see me? Can you prove it?" By this time I was laughing so hard, tears were forming around my eyes from the hilarity. I was thinking that if this could have been caught on film, Lora could have sent it off to America's Funniest Home Videos and have had a decent chance at the prize. Of course then Lora came back into the building with the other handlers and the entertainment portion of the class was over, but Ranger had won a spot in my heart.

"Happy Ranger"

As time went by and I got to know Ranger better, I knew I had to try to get the opportunity to tell his gatekeeper story. Aside from a few superficial things, I didn't know much about Australian Shepherds at all. The first thing I learned from Ranger's demonstration was that Australian Shepherds, and certainly including Ranger, are clearly not to be underestimated. Lora relayed a story to me about one day when she had a friend over visiting with her dogs. They were all out in the backyard enjoying the day, and the dogs were playing together without issue for a while when Lora noticed that Ranger was starting to get a little snippy with the other dogs. So she separated him from the others by placing him in an xpen, which is a little enclosed gated area. The height of the pen is low and Ranger could easily have jumped it. However, he knows that jumping out of the pen is not allowed. Therein was the dilemma. How could he get back to playing with the others without being disobedient?

Photo by Steve Southard Photography

Ranger had been confined to the pen maybe seven or eight minutes, clearly enough time to think this problem through, when to Lora's surprise, she saw Ranger jump from within the pen up onto the adjacent barbecue and from there make his way down to where the other dogs were playing. No problem here. He must have left the snippy attitude in the pen because the rest of the day passed without issue. Ranger is clearly a dog who never sees himself as out of options.

It's amazing how resourceful Ranger continues to be. When I was visiting with Lora in preparation for this story, the first thing that I noticed was that the alarm was sounded by the dogs when I arrived. However, as soon as Lora invited me in, Ranger looked at me as if to say, "Hey, I remember you, you love me, and I just bet you brought treats." I was starting to see a trend here. First Lulu, now Ranger. Do these dogs know I'm a soft touch or what?! Without waiting for an invitation, he stuck his nose right into my purse, wiggling his nose around till he moved the zipper enough to find the treats. As I watched him do this, most of his head disappeared into the bag, and I figured I'd better get the treats out before there was dog drool all over my possessions. (Not that Ranger would drool). Ranger seemed to think this was a great idea since he wouldn't have to work as hard to get the goodies. I got them out, and as I stood up, I found myself face to face with Ranger who had absolutely no problem jumping straight up in the air to help himself to the treat in my hand. At this point, I found myself wondering if Ranger and Kobe were somehow related because sneaking treats from unsuspecting people was definitely a Kobe trick. So it appears to also be a Ranger trick.

As we were visiting, Lora showed me one of Ranger's favorite toys called a jolly ball. Ranger enjoys having his jolly ball wherever he is so leaving it outside when he's inside is not a doable situation. For those of you who may not know what a jolly ball is, it's a very durable rubber type ball that comes in different sizes and with a handle on it. Ranger has a big jolly ball and with a ball that size, it's a challenge to move it inside or outside when one is going in and out through a doggie door. So one day Ranger decided to see if he could solve this dilemma. The most obvious tactic would be to try and push it through from the outside. After all, his weight would be behind him so it makes sense, right? After trying with all diligence to push it through but without success, he decided maybe trying to pull it through might be a viable alternative. It's got a handle on it that must be good for something other than playing tug of war with mom. So Ranger came in through the doggie door, turned around, put his head through the door, grabbed the handle and pulled and pulled some more until, Voila! there came the jolly ball through the doggie door. He was so proud of himself.

Ranger with his jolly ball

Not long ago, much to Ranger's dismay, his nephew Scout became a part of the family. Scout is also a blue merle male and though he is a puppy, he is already living up to his uncle's legacy. Lora brings Scout to class too and uses him as well for age appropriate demonstrations. Scout has his uncle's exuberance, and he apparently doesn't appreciate being left in his xpen while everyone else is out on the floor working and/or playing. Like Ranger, Scout knows he's not allowed to jump out of the pen. One night as Lora was busy teaching the class, I was working Kobe when I heard a weird sound behind me. I glanced back just in time to see Scout move the entire xpen with him in our direction. He had his head down and like a little Billy goat was pushing the pen to where he wanted to go. Naturally, Lora moved the pen back to its original location but already I could see Scout's brain working as if to say, "Ah nuts . . . there's always next time." Our pets can be such great friends, who are also wildly entertaining!

As you can see from Ranger's titles behind his name, he is an extremely accomplished, advanced level working dog. If you're interested in knowing what all of those letters mean, they can be found on the AKC website under obedience working titles. While this story was not designed to talk about all of Ranger's accomplishments, I would be remiss to not mention that Ranger was invited to the AKC National Obedience Invitational (NOI) that was held March 2013 in Oklahoma. In order to get invited to the NOI you have to qualify at a regional event or have the top 10 OTCH (Obedience Trial Champion) points in your breed. Lora and Ranger qualified after a great weekend they had at the Truckee Meadows Trials that was a regional event in July of 2012. Ranger also qualified to enter the AKC Obedience Classic in Utility being held in December of 2013 in Florida, due to his scores in the previous year in Utility. He had also qualified for the ASCA (Australian Shepherd Club of America) Obedience finals the last two years in a row that are held at the ASCA National. At the time of this writing, Ranger is only two points away from his AKC Herding Championship. The list of titles behind Ranger's name on the first page of this story represents the highest level in each venue: Obedience, Tracking, Rally, Agility, Herding, and Versatility. Ranger deserves high praise and recognition for all that he has done. But even more for what he is, a loving companion who is very smart with a great sense of humor and who brings great joy to his family and to all who know him.

Ranger and Lora TDX—Photo by Donna Highstreet

Chapter 15

Koa

Life is so much more fun when you have a best friend to share it with. Koa is that for Kobe. Koa is a five-year-old male boxer. On weekend mornings Erick normally takes Kobe for an early morning run to a particular park, and when Kobe was still a young puppy, they met Pete and Koa there and a friendship was born. It wasn't long before we also met Jenni, Pete's wife, and their sons, Jayk, Peter, and Matthew.

I'm always interested to know why someone chooses a particular dog, so I asked Jenni why she wanted a boxer as opposed to another breed of dog. She said she was always attracted to the cute pug face that she thought was so adorable, and wanted a dog that was short-haired and didn't shed much. She liked how Boxers were notorious for being silly and light hearted, "the clown," and full of fun. She also wanted an athletic dog that could keep up with an active family. She found Koa to be those things and so much more. Jenni said that Koa is the most patient and tolerant dog she's ever known.

Koa came home with the family when he was ten weeks old. He was one of a litter of five, a big boy with a black face, just as Jenni had imagined. From the start everyone in the family thought Koa was so cuddly and sweet and appreciated how he always wanted to be with the family. The boys wanted to make sure that Koa didn't feel lonely and scared being away from his littermates for the first time, so they asked their mom if they could have Koa sleep upstairs with them in their room. Jenni said, "No, but if you would like, you can sleep with Koa downstairs in your sleeping bags." As I was conducting this interview, I then turned to the boys and asked them which one(s) of them slept downstairs with the dog. They looked at each other and finally said, "All of us." So I followed that up with, "That must have made Koa's first days in his new home wonderful and comforting. So how long did you sleep downstairs with him?" I got only silence from the boys, so Jenni quipped in, "A year and a half!" I about fell out of my chair laughing, but I said, "I'm not laughing at you. I'm laughing because this would have been a common occurrence at my house, so I understand perfectly." At first Koa was new but after that, he was just loved that much.

Koa has a great life and is always a happy dog, which the boys appreciate so much about him. Pete works, but Jenni and the boys are usually home since the boys are home schooled. They also do activities with other home-schooled students, and Koa has become the home schooling mascot. Koa is well socialized and gets to go to a local park every Wednesday to be with his home-schooled friends. When

Jenni, the kids, and Koa arrive, the teens usually take Koa for a long walk to the end of the park and back. He's also been known to play field games with the kids, however this can get tricky since Koa has to be kept on leash. In addition, the students have their annual Halloween and Valentine's Day parties at the park and of course, Koa is always invited. Most often, he is simply dressed in a bandana of the appropriate color, but he's been known to dress up too. He's loved and is quite popular with his young friends. I can imagine that Koa just melts at the thought of being petted and played with by a whole group of students. Tough job but someone's got to do it. At home he also has Pete, who enjoys walking with him, and apparently Pete also enjoys Koa as his wrestling buddy. Talk about a well-rounded life for a dog.

Jenni mentioned that while Koa also has other dogs he occasionally plays with, apparently Koa is as fond of Kobe as Kobe is of him. In fact, when I went over to Pete and Jenni's to do this interview, Koa met me at the door with excitement, clearly glad to see me. That was until he realized I hadn't brought Kobe. He kept looking around past me to my car as if to say, "Hey, where's Kobe? You didn't come without him, did you?" I told him, "Next time, buddy, I'll bring Kobe along."

Even though it's a "guys' time," one weekend I went with Erick so I could see for myself Koa and Kobe together.

"Cool Koa"

This was when I hadn't yet officially met Koa. I haven't known many Dobermans that can run with other adult males, especially big ones, and do consistently well. When Kobe and Koa first saw each other at the park, they first stopped as if to acknowledge the other's presence. Then they moved forward towards each other a little bit and then stopped again. They may have done this one additional time before they finally ran straight towards each other and greeted each other with little jumps and yips before running off together side by side in tandem as if they had been doing this all their lives. It was amazing. They didn't quarrel over things they found but would share, an amazing concept for dogs.

"Koa and Kobe Running Free"

And it wasn't just that one time; they've been running together regularly now for probably close to two years. Koa and Kobe running together can seem like an intimidating sight, especially to other people coming to the park with their dogs. But even after all this time there have been no issues other than the occasional grumbling from the other dogs' owners. Of course Erick and Pete are always close by and maintain excellent control of the dogs.

Once we had Koa stay with us for a day while Pete and Jenni and the family had a chance to get away. At first I was concerned, because running together on neutral ground was one thing, now they would be on Kobe's home territory. But it was a fun day for all of us. At one point in the afternoon, I was out in our backyard with both dogs, and I saw them stop in front of each other face to face. It probably wasn't for more than a minute, but they took turns woofing at each other, not really barking, just communicating. I was trying to imagine what they might be saying and all I could come up with was, Koa: "Okay, we've already been on two walks and have played ball. So what do you want to do now?" Kobe: "Oh, I don't know. You want to dig up one of my bones? I actually have a couple, enough for both of us." Koa: "How about doing that after a nap? I'm tired." Kobe: "Good idea!" After that, they laid down on the lawn and slept. I wanted to grab my camera and take a picture of this discourse between them but had already learned that if I move, the dogs move with me. When it was dinner time, Koa and Kobe acted just like siblings. I fixed them both an excellent dinner, each in their own bowls at different, though nearby, places so there would be no argument. They each sniffed their own dinner and then promptly went over and heartily ate the other dog's meal. Both dogs contented. No problem here.

As I shared this talk our dogs had with Jenni, she told me that on occasion, Koa does talk. While I believed her, I had a hard time visualizing it other than the woofing I heard between Kobe and him, so she and the kids called Koa over and told him to say "Mama." As they continued to encourage him to talk, Koa started to warm up his vocal chords very much like a singer may wish to warm up before a performance. It was hard not to giggle but I was trying hard not to distract him in any way from his task. And sure enough, after duly clearing his voice, he said, "Mama." He even said something after that that sounded very much like "I love you." I think both statements, if you can call them that, were clear enough for most anyone to understand. What a character!

Koa has lots of other fun pastimes, like sleeping (yes, I noticed that), running (goes without saying), being petted (probably close to the top of the list), and going for rides anywhere—even to places like Lowes or Home Depot. He makes friends everywhere he goes, so why not? Koa has a way of convincing one to play with him. If members of his family aren't paying attention to him quickly enough, he has been known to poke at them on the rear end if they're standing or on the back of the neck if it's reachable. He's not particular except to say that he wants some attention NOW and maybe to stir up the pot a little bit.

It's not always just playtime with Koa. He likes to go camping, picnicking, and hiking with the Boy Scout troop that the boys are a part of. He has his own red backpack so he can carry some of the things he'll need for the hike. One time as the group was hiking, they came across a calf. The calf and Koa seemed to be equally curious about each other, however mama cow intervened by going between Koa and the calf. She then had a stare down with Koa as if to say, "Don't mess with my baby." This probably lasted for only a minute, which doesn't sound like a long time, but it sure seemed like it. The whole troop stood and watched, frozen, afraid to move, wondering what would happen. Nothing happened as Koa wisely returned to the group and mama was just as happy not to have to defend her baby.

Koa's greatest desire and need is to be with the family, not just for all the fun but also to take his place making a functional contribution to their well-being. He always lays where he can see everyone and what they are doing. Jayk has grand mall seizures. When Jayk has a seizure, Koa will be right there beside him. Jayk may sometimes be passed out for six or seven hours. During that time, Koa may get up to eat or go outside to take care of important business, but will always keep coming back and checking on Jayk and does not seem to completely relax until he knows that all is well.

Some of his tasks are more light-hearted. The family has a turtle named Salona that lives outside. When the family cannot find Salona, they send Koa to find her. And find her he does, and is always gentle with her. Once Koa found her inside a bush, and over time, Koa, much better than the family, has learned where Salona's favorite hiding places are. I imagine that Koa knows her scent and uses that to find her. I'd ask him if that's how he does it, but I'm not sure Koa would share his secret.

Koa is also a proven gatekeeper. He barks when strangers come near to their home alerting the family to someone's presence, and with Koa's face appearing next to the door, I don't imagine many people would even consider taking him on. Koa sometimes also intervenes between family members but when that happens, it's instigated by the family. They think it's funny how Koa will protect Jenni from Pete and protect the boys from Jenni. Jenni thought that in the beginning, it was a "size thing,"—that Koa would protect the smaller one, but now she's not so sure. The boys are so tall .. . Jenni's thinking that it might be all about Koa and his boys.

Koa is obviously family in every way. In front of their home, Pete and Jenni have a place for visitors to leave their shoes in order to keep the house cleaner. Well Koa obviously has no shoes to remove so he does the next best thing. There is a towel kept by the door and when Koa comes in, one of the family will count from one to four. When they count "one," Koa lifts one front paw to be cleaned. "Two," and he lifts his other front paw. "Three" and "four" are said for the back paws, which Koa dutifully lifts when the number is called. What a good boy!!

Koa has added to our lives too. Erick continues to take Kobe to meet Pete and Koa for their early morning runs on most weekends, and I enjoy Koa so much every time I see him and get to play with him. But I'm especially grateful that Kobe has such a good friend that is a consistent part of his life. Whether warranted or not, most people go to great lengths to keep their dogs away from Kobe. But to see two friends like Kobe and Koa welcome each other always with such freedom, familiarity, and joy is one of my life's sweet pleasures.

"Forever Friends"

Chapter 16

Rocket

Zamora's Reach for the Stars
RE, BN, MXJB, MX, T2B, XF, CA, CGC

David and Goliath. That's the impression I got when I saw my Kobe and Rocket standing nose to nose the other night in class, after not having seen each other for almost a year. Except in this case Goliath is a good guy who likes David and obviously enjoys the friendship. Rocket is a seven and a half pound, black toy poodle to Kobe's ninety pounds of black Doberman. An interesting sight. As I've shared before, I've never been much of a poodle fan as I've regarded the majority of them as over-pampered, high-strung, temperamental dogs. Rocket is none of the above. He is smart, solid, even tempered, and as far as I've seen, afraid of nothing. And he's not one of those little dogs that tries to challenge dogs that are many times their size in order to prove something. Rocket is calm and confident, which is very admirable. I would have thought that Rocket would be a weird name for a toy poodle; that is until I saw him respond to a recall command. I'm not certain that his feet even touched the ground even though they obviously must have. Watching Rocket work is a privilege.

"Rocket over jump"—Photo by Bruce A. McClelland

Rocket and Kobe met when they were in the same Show Novice class. One of my favorite memories so far of Rocket was one night when we were waiting for class to begin. Marla Marlow, Rocket's owner and number one fan, was teaching Rocket to speak. She had Rocket's treat in her hand and was repeatedly saying, "Rocket, speak!" It was hit and miss at the time, so I had the bright idea that Kobe might be able to help. So I said, "Kobe, speak!" And speak he did; in fact, I couldn't get Kobe to shut up. Every time Marla told Rocket to speak, Kobe answered. I don't know if Kobe thought that Marla would give him the treat or not, but it occurred to me that maybe I should have kept my bright idea to myself. At one point, Rocket looked at Kobe as if to say, "Is your name Rocket??" He was so incredibly cute!

Rocket is almost four years old now. Marla also has a much older toy poodle named Rio and a Shar-pei named

Kobe. (The only other dog named Kobe that I've ever met.) Marla had been a Shar-pei breeder for years, so I asked her why she considered getting not only one toy poodle but two of them. Marla said she got the poodles because they're small, smart, clean, don't shed, and are willing to please.

Photo by Dave Nash

Rocket may want to please, but like most dogs he can be just like a little kid sometimes. They're wonderful and well behaved until you have company. And then they try to test their limits and see just how much they can get away with. While I was visiting Marla and her dogs for this interview, Rocket was about as mischievous as a little dog can get. He often didn't come when called, and instead, he enjoyed jumping around behind me on the couch, climbing on my back, clawing and biting my sweater, chewing on my hair, and jumping over my hand as I was trying to type, leaving a row of interesting nonsense letters across the page. But he really was cute, and he knew it. Actually, I think Rocket was just jealous because Marla had the other poodle in her lap. Regardless of these brief lapses of good judgment, Rocket is a very good working dog and when he has his head in the game, he can be show stopping fun to watch. He already has titles in agility, basic rally, and basic obedience, to mention a few. I'm not sure that there is anything Rocket can't do if he sets his mind to it.

Looking at Rocket now, it's hard to imagine that he was afraid of people when Marla first got him. Clearly, Marla has given him a lot of love and attention because Rocket has totally overcome his fear and is about as secure as any little dog I've ever seen. He didn't just overcome his fear of people but fear of anything. From the first time I met him, Rocket went right up to my Kobe and made friends, no problem. If I recall correctly, I think Marla had some concerns about her seven and a half pound poodle approaching a Doberman without reservation. But all was well and has remained well. During the process of my interview with Marla, I saw Rocket wrestling around on the floor with the Shar-pei (Kobe), and I winced a time or two when Rocket was on the bottom with Kobe on top and they were moving fast and hard, but there's no question that this is something that they do often and enjoy tremendously.

Marla told me of a time when she was temperament testing a litter of Rottweiler puppies. In addition to the usual tests, the "poodle test" was added to see how the puppies reacted to him. After all, Rocket is a very little poodle probably not all that much bigger than the puppies. As Marla was describing this testing procedure to me, I envisioned Rocket playing with a puppy or two at a time, and I could see Rocket thinking that this was a lot of fun, playing with other dogs that were for a change smaller than he was. Quite a novelty. My vision came to an abrupt halt when Marla said that at one point, she put Rocket in with all eleven puppies at the same time. ELEVEN Rottweiler puppies and one little toy poodle, and Rocket was fine and he loved it. This is one little dog with guts!

Rocket is not only mostly fearless, he is inventive. He can do a lot of tricks like twirling, jumping up into Marla's arms on command, asking for treats from either a standing or sitting position, will jump over the Shar-pei who remains standing, and is always learning more. All good tricks that make poodles adorable. However, he does have some tricks that he was not taught and that are not always approved of. For instance, he is an escape artist, always climbing out of things that he is supposed to remain in, like an xpen. He'll use his claws, his teeth, whatever is needed. I wonder if Marla ever has to remind Rocket that he's a poodle.

Rocket lure coursing—Photo by Jason Largent

The evidence would seem to indicate that Rocket sees himself at least as part hound dog when he runs. And Rocket can run, not just run like other poodles I've seen, I mean RUN! This little dog can fly at lure coursing events that are made available for non-hunting dogs. (I couldn't imagine it, but it's true nonetheless.) In other words, he doesn't run with the sight and scent hounds like the Ridgebacks as described in Joie's chapter, but regardless, Rocket is the real deal as you can see in the photo.

But Rocket is so much more than the working dog or a cute little dog that does tricks. Marla describes him as a very loving dog with a lot of stamina, always ready to go and do whatever Marla wants to do. She takes him hiking in the parks, they go to the beach, and because he's so well socialized, she can take him almost anywhere. He's good with people and with other dogs. When he quit showing off for me while I was visiting, he came and sat in my lap and gave me kisses. Rocket has a very sweet and compassionate nature. Marla says that she calls him Dr. Dog. If Rocket senses that someone or even another dog is in distress, he'll want to fix it and make it better. He'll do this by barking his empathy or by licking a wound until he seems convinced that the injured party is better. As Marla was describing this to me, I realized that Rocket was licking my finger where there had been a recent blister. The blister was already healed, but apparently Rocket felt that the area still needed a little more TLC. This gesture of kindness from this dog was just precious.

At home, Rocket of course enjoys wrestling with the Shar-pei, playing with his toys, and also enjoys watching television. Not the boring shows, but he watches videos of himself doing agility events, or other dog shows that he can really get into. And like Phoenix, he will bark at the appropriate times to punctuate the action. I'm thinking that probably half the time Marla enjoys watching him as much as she enjoys the show itself.

Rocket also has his favorite pastimes. I think at some level most if not all dogs have vices in common. One of Rocket's is chasing squirrels. He is so prey driven (the lure coursing now makes sense) that Marla won't have him off leash in some public areas where he is likely to come across squirrels close enough to be chased, because he's liable to just take off and not come back until he's either caught or lost his prey. Reminds me of Joie and my Kobe! It occurred to me that any squirrel being chased by a Rhodesian Ridgeback (Joie) or a Doberman (Kobe) would have just cause for alarm because these are big dogs. But might a squirrel be saying, upon looking at little Rocket, "You think you can catch me? I don't think so." Boy would that squirrel be in for a surprise! Rocket is very much at home in the outdoors. He won't just chase squirrels either. He's been known to also chase birds and deer. In fact, one time he took off after a deer and apparently stopped at nothing because after getting home, Marla spent four and a half hours getting all the burrs and stickers out of Rocket's fur. That's commitment both on Rocket's part and also on Marla's.

Rocket doesn't just like to chase animals that run (or fly) free. Once Marla took him along when she was going to a herding lesson with her Kobe. Rocket may have been maybe two years old at the time but made it clear that he was ready for any and all challenges. As he watched Kobe learning to herd sheep, he obviously must have said to himself, "If Kobe can do this, I can do this." Rocket made enough noise that Marla let him out of the car and off Rocket went; the chase was on. There Rocket was, all seven and a half pounds of him, trying to herd probably a half dozen Barbados sheep, each of them weighing up to two hundred pounds. Rocket was barking, ears flying, enjoying a little adventure with sheer exhilaration. I can just imagine that the sheep may have been saying, "Is that little thing running behind us for real?" Rocket may never be a working herding dog but his efforts were rewarded when one of the sheep came over to him and gave him a good-sized lick. And Rocket, of course, being the sweetie that he usually is, gave the sheep a little kiss in return.

Rocket doesn't just enjoy parks but also loves the beach. Marla said the first time she took Rocket to the beach, he loved it so much that he just took off running in the sand until he was out of sight. She became concerned that he might get hurt by other animals or get swept away by the ocean waves, but lo and behold, she finally saw him running back to her; running like the wind, free as a bird. Since then, when they've gone to the beach, Rocket stays closer, still running, but sometimes just bouncing up and down next to her with excitement. One time, Rocket got bit by a crab which he took very personally (who wouldn't?). Since then, crabs seem to be on his public enemy number one list. If he sees one, it's attack first and ask questions later. Rocket, yes, little Rocket has absolutely no problem striking first by pulling the crab's legs off one by one till the crab can no longer move. Self-preservation is very important.

Rocket doesn't just protect himself. When I arrived for my visit, he ran right in front of me barking with as much emphasis as is possible from a little dog. And I must admit, that was quite a bit. When I tried to move forward toward the house, Rocket starting running around me, almost like a herding dog, trying to keep me away. He continued his vigil until Marla came and got him and said it was okay. Even after that, he wasn't too sure until we all settled down in the living room. Marla said that Kobe was the watchdog but it seems Rocket has decided to give him a hand.

Recently a man came to do a perimeter inspection of the house. He came through the side gate, and Kobe was out there to protect his yard. This lasted until the man reached down to touch Kobe, which Kobe didn't like so he took off. Rocket, sensing Kobe's anxiety, decided it was his turn and took off after the man. Little or not, Rocket can be very convincing as I learned firsthand. Between the three dogs, who all love and care for Marla, I don't think she need have any concern about being loved and protected. Clearly, gatekeepers come in small sizes and assorted shapes, but their commitment, loyalty, and determination to protect home and loved ones are just as great.

Chapter 17

Purr-fect Feline Gatekeepers

You may very well be thinking that it's strange, not to mention totally weird, having a feline chapter in this book. However, there is irrefutable evidence that there are felines that have done some incredible things to protect themselves and their loved ones. I feel most privileged to share a few of their stories.

Mocha

Mocha is a ten-year-old, eleven pound Siamese cross cat belonging to Steve and Charlotte Stevenson. She originally became a part of the family when Steve and Charlotte's daughter, Julie, adopted her. Mocha was a stray—very thin, and also very pregnant at the time. Though she'd shown herself to be a very independent cat, Mocha was smart enough to know she had found a loving home. However, Julie was in the army and when she was transferred to South Korea, Mocha went to live with Steve and Charlotte. This would become most fortuitous in light of what Mocha would come to mean to them.

Mocha with Steve and Charlotte

Mocha is a gentle cat that enjoys her peaceful leisurely naps. She doesn't however want to miss anything exciting happening, so she can often be found following Steve around very much like a puppy might. Like most cats she enjoys an occasional hunt especially if she can find grasshoppers to play with. In other words, she's a normal cat but one that is very sensitive to the well-being of her family.

Charlotte has been diabetic for thirty-seven years and has been on insulin for thirty-three years. One particular incident happened about five years ago. Normally Steve is very sensitive to Charlotte and her well-being; however, he had just returned from Alaska and was exhausted after the long trip. So very early one morning when Mocha jumped up on the bed and meowed continually into Steve's ear, he automatically assumed that she was either hungry or needed to go out and sleepily started moving towards her food in the kitchen. But before long he realized that Mocha was not with him and went back into the bedroom. Mocha had stayed with Charlotte, and that was when Steve realized that something was very wrong. Steve tried to wake her, but Charlotte was unresponsive. She was sweating profusely even though the covers had been thrown back and soon Steve recognized that she was, in fact, unconscious. Steve immediately tested her blood and got a reading of 13, a reading that indicated she was in diabetic shock.

As calmly as was possible, Steve went to get Charlotte's medication and injected her with glucagon. It usually takes about ten minutes for the medication to do its job. Ten minutes probably seemed like much longer as Steve fervently prayed that Charlotte would recover. As Charlotte started to come around, Steve made sure she had juice to drink that would further bring up and balance her blood glucose levels. In about an hour and a half, Charlotte's condition had improved to the point where she could be considered functional. Mocha had stayed with Charlotte the entire time. Had Mocha not awakened Steve with her persistent meowing, Charlotte would likely not have survived the night.

Mocha has never given up keeping her vigil. Just a week and a half prior to this writing, Mocha once again let her meow sound the alarm that Charlotte's blood sugar was once again too low. Mocha somehow just knows and can sense when Charlotte is not well. I imagine that to Steve and Charlotte and their family, they have been sent a guardian angel in the form of a sweet and loving cat.

Sammie

You briefly met Sammie in Benji and Justin's story as she liked to go hiking with us and the dogs in the park. As previously mentioned, the only time we had to carry her was when the trail crossed the Van Duzen River. Swimming was not her thing at all, but if we left her, she would meow loudly until we went back to get her. Otherwise, she hiked right along with us, undeterred in her quest to prove she could do whatever the dogs could do.

I had had cats as I was growing up, and when I saw the litter of kittens born to a friend's cat, I couldn't resist. Samantha, Sammie for short, was a sweet little calico, and I thought the timing was perfect as she would grow up with Benji and Justin. I've always considered it risky and unwise to bring a cat into a family with adult dogs. It often does not turn out well.

She remained a small cat even as an adult, but as small as she was, she had so much heart and turned out to be a force to be reckoned with. She moved with us out into Van Duzen County Park where Erick was the resident ranger. Out in the woods, cats face obstacles that they generally don't in the city, like deer, owls, wild rabbits, raccoons, skunks, squirrels . . . actually, squirrels are everywhere. I was concerned for her well-being and tried making her into an indoor cat but alas, Sammie liked to hunt.

One time we saw Sammie chase a rat (that looked to be bigger than she was) up a redwood tree. But catch it she did and dragged that rat all thirty or forty feet back down the tree and presented it to us as a precious gift. Gross . . . but she had no shame and no fear. That rat did turn out to be bigger than she was, and she also caught others and thought it special to bring them home to share. Really gross. She didn't limit herself to rats but caught birds and what-ever else she could catch up to. What I always thought was really funny was that when she got in over her head with some animal, she would run for home in a hurry, jump over the fence, and let Benji and Justin protect her—and she would smugly watch. One smart cat!

That doesn't mean she wasn't a fighter, she was. Sammie never went looking for trouble but if trouble found her, she was up to the task. The absolute proof of this was demonstrated one evening as we were returning home from an outing. Sammie ran out to greet us, but as she was passing across the driveway, a huge owl swooped down and picked Sammie up and carried her away. We heard her screaming as she passed over our boundary fence and into the night. It happened so quickly and so unexpectedly that there was nothing we could do. I burst into tears and ran to the fence to see if I could follow where the owl went. But it was already too dark. We were heartbroken and considered losing Sammie a tragic loss.

A while later that evening as we sat at the kitchen table reminiscing about our adventurous cat, we heard a meow at the door and thought surely we must be imagining it. But we ran to the door and there Sammie stood, ruffled and scratched, but otherwise whole. She jumped into our arms and we hugged and kissed her and Benji and Justin welcomed her back too. We have no idea how she escaped, as owls are tenacious predators with long talons, the evidence of which was streaked across Sammie's back. We watched her carefully but she recovered well. She seemed to stay a little closer to home after that for a while and closer to the dogs when she was out, but she never lost her spirit.

While she likely thought she was one of the dogs (she slept with Justin in his house), she was smart and did not partake when Benji and Justin ate the rabbit skins. I don't know if cats can laugh or not, but Sammie sure seemed to have a smirk on her face.

After we moved to Concord, Sammie made the transition well. She continued to sleep with Justin and felt right at home. Sammie was so comfortable with big dogs that she had no issue whatsoever when Rischa as a young puppy came to live with us. In fact, Rischa was very protective, something Sammie totally appreciated and took utmost advantage of when other animals chased her. Sammie was a great cat, wonderful with our children when they were born, and all her days remained part of the "Doberman gang." We have always considered ourselves very lucky to have had such an amazing cat as part of our family.

Sammie with Erick and Bryan

Cassie

You met Cassie in JT's story. This was the loving cat that JT tracked and found after she had been missing for many months. But her story began much earlier. Cassie was another calico kitten. This should have forewarned me that we might have adopted another scrapper into the family. Cassie belonged to my daughter, Erin, and came to live with us some time after we lost Robin. This made Cassie hard for me to like at first because she was a reminder that my sweet Robin was gone. But as time went by, Cassie grew on me, and before I knew it, she was so sweet and loving that it became easy for me to love her.

One of my first unique memories of Cassie was one night when she was still a young kitten. Cassie stayed with Erin and our grandson, Josh, in their room, which was at one end of our upstairs landing. Our master bedroom was at the other end of the landing with a small bedroom/office and a hall bathroom in between. I had just kissed Erin and Josh goodnight and was returning to my bedroom for the night. Before closing the master bedroom door, I briefly glanced back and saw Cassie quietly sitting adjacent to Josh's crib. So I turned back around and shut the master bedroom door and that instant heard a loud "thunk."

I reopened the door to see Cassie lying there next to the door, and I imagined seeing little birds flying in a circle around her head as she tried to regain her composure, not to mention her balance. The only possible explanation that we could come up with was that the minute I turned my back, little Miss Cassie charged, positioned to attack and pounce on me. (I so wish that could somehow have been caught on film.) She clearly was coming way too fast to stop when I closed the door. Though she did her share of pouncing after that, interestingly enough, she never challenged me at any door ever again that I can remember. Smart girl. Smart and fast and definitely sneaky.

One evening when Cassie was twelve weeks old, we were watching a program in the living room and Erick was helping himself to a soup snack right out of the can. Cassie must have thought that it smelled wonderful because she curled up on Erick's arm and tried to sneak a snack right out from under his nose. When Erick tried to move the can out of her way, Cassie went right after it. This cat wouldn't take no for an answer. Cassie snuck a few bites right off

Erick's spoon (told you she was fast), and when Erick finished the soup Cassie crawled right into the can and proceeded to lick up any remaining bits.

Cassie and Erick

Cassie was a young adult cat when I brought JT home.
She was in quite a snit at first, but once she got used to
him, she was just annoyed. She liked to bathe herself, thank
you, and did not appreciate it when JT would come up to
her and lick her. She seemed to find it necessary to re-lick
every part of her that JT touched. She turned out to be a
consistently very clean cat.

Dog or no dog, Cassie remained very much at home at
our house. Cassie, like Sammie, was very adaptable and
moved with Erin and Josh easily. Cassie knew the sound of
my car, and often when I would visit, she would hear my
car and come running in greeting. I'd open my car door
and she would jump into the car and then onto my lap for
some undivided attention, petting, and love before I could

go in the house. The big exception of course was when I had JT with me. JT never could understand why Cassie didn't appreciate his company as much as he enjoyed hers.

Cassie liked her new home and found a wonderful place to habitually sit on the counter next to the center window in the kitchen. She enjoyed that spot even though Erin, as a rule, discouraged her presence on the counter. For one thing, if she was already up there, it would be too easy for her to swipe food, and swipe food she would if she got the chance.

One morning, Erick and I had been invited to Erin's for breakfast. Erin had a bowl of sliced cantaloupe on the counter while preparing the rest of the meal. None of us had any idea that Cassie liked cantaloupe, but what she did next eliminated any doubt. In the blink of an eye, Cassie made a mad dash for the bowl and with one swipe of her paw snagged a slice of cantaloupe which found its way onto the floor. Cassie of course jumped right after it, grabbed it, and hightailed it down the hall with her catch. The next time we saw her, she was licking her paw with great satisfaction.

Cassie didn't just settle for what she could swipe, aside from her regular food. She acquired a taste for humming-bird. They're fast too, but sometimes Cassie was faster. There was a corner of Erin's yard that had a lovely rose bush. Cassie would make herself really small hiding beneath the bush and when the hummingbirds would come to feed on the adjacent plants, she would pounce. She caught six hummingbirds that Erin knew of, which was always sad. Couldn't really blame Cassie for doing what came to her instinctively, but it was sad nonetheless.

Cassie, like Sammie, was a born hunter. When Cassie was still living at our house, she took on a possum and killed it. Between first Robin and then Cassie, I would have thought that cats and other animals would spread the word among themselves that our yard was not one they wanted to get caught in. And Cassie really needed to go outside and hunt. If Erin tried to keep her inside, she would get very antsy and start attacking feet the minute they hit the floor in the morning. Or she would pounce on you when you crossed a threshold. In other words, she would hunt one way or the other. So out she went. This is how Cassie came to be lost when she moved with Erin to the condo. She survived on her own for eight months before JT tracked and found her. We considered Cassie a most loving, one-in-a-million cat with amazing survival skills. Cassie was unforgettable in every way.

Chapter 18

Sharp

When I first heard about Sharp, I was trying to remember what I knew about English Mastiffs. Other than they were big dogs originally from England, I basically knew nothing. I don't think I had ever even seen one up close and personal. So before I met with Sharp and his owners, Sunny and Genia Armas, I decided to do a little research. The first sentence of their online description was that English Mastiffs are "distinguishable by their enormous size and massive head always displaying a black mask and noted for their gentle temperament. They are the largest breed of dog in terms of their mass."

I've had large dogs for close to forty years, so I'm thinking, *how big can they be*? The minute I arrived at the Armas home, my first impression was that the internet is maybe more accurate than I had given it credit for. Sunny and Sharp were in the front yard as I pulled up, and I thought that maybe in the dark with inadequate lighting, Sharp might be able to pass for a small bear. Certainly big enough for my three-year-old granddaughter to ride on. Not that I would ever let her. I learned that Sharp is about 180 pounds, and some English Mastiffs get to be as big as

250 pounds. But I have to say that as big as Sharp is, his heart is bigger, and he is smart. As soon as Sunny told Sharp that I was an invited guest and not an unwelcome stranger, Sharp was immediately at ease.

Sharp is now four years old but came to live with Sunny and Genia when he was seven months old. The Armases had owned English Mastiffs before, and they were all loved, but they were quick to say that there was clearly an "inseparable love affair" between Sunny and Sharp. Years ago, Sunny had suffered a traumatic brain injury resulting from a motorcycle accident. Even though much healing has taken place, Sunny still suffers from seizure-like migraine headaches that leave him debilitated for sometimes days or weeks at a time.

Sharp with Sunny and Genia

From the time Sharp was young, he would without any warning come to Sunny and persistently nudge him, sit next to him, paw and whine, put his head in Sunny's lap, basically do whatever he had to do to get Sunny's undivided attention. Most dogs do that with their owners to one degree or another, but it wasn't long before Sunny and Genia both realized that the extent to which Sharp was insisting on this attention came approximately ten to fifteen minutes before an onset of one of Sunny's seizure-like migraine headaches. If Sunny would immediately take his medication before the onset of the attack, he could avoid the terribly painful aftermath. This incredible dog, without any training, could somehow instinctively sense when Sunny was about to have an attack. I can easily understand the strength of the bond between Sunny and Sharp, and because of Sharp's amazing instincts and proven capabilities, he has become licensed as a service dog.

To add to the drama, Sunny suffered a stroke on January 8, 2013, and was hospitalized for two days in the intensive care unit and then in the coronary care unit of Kaiser Santa Clara. Sunny's blood pressure would skyrocket but would drop to within safe parameters when Sharp was brought to him. Because Sharp was a service dog, he was allowed to stay in a special bed made up for him there in Sunny's room next to him. Sharp made it clear that anyone who came into Sunny's room would have to greet him first or he would not permit them to go to Sunny. He would otherwise bark a very clear "don't approach" message. Sharp placed himself as a barrier between Sunny and other people and seemed to have a clear sense of who was safe and who wasn't.

Specifically, because he learns quickly what behaviors are appropriate and normal within a certain setting or environment, Sharp knew what the doctors and nurses did as part of Sunny's required care. He learned this from Sunny's approval and his telling Sharp that the behavior was okay. If someone deviated from those behaviors when approaching

Sunny, Sharp alerted and didn't allow the person to proceed until Sunny told him it was okay, and that Sharp could relax.

On the lighter side, Sharp still had the same needs that all dogs have, so periodically he would need to be taken outside to do his "chores." Genia was the only one Sharp would allow to take him from Sunny's presence. However he did not appreciate having a leash put on him so he decided he could hold Genia's hand instead much like a child will hold an adult's hand, only of course he did this with his mouth. I saw the size of this dog's mouth and also all the slobber in it, and I was trying to imagine what that sight might have looked like … and I decided it looked quite precious. But it was also very funny and very human-like, and I wish I had a picture of it. One of these days, I may work up the nerve to ask Sunny and Genia if Sharp might be willing to take me on a short walk. Some things in life just have to be experienced. Sharp apparently never left so much as a tooth mark on Genia's hand, and she was happy to take him out. Absolutely amazing!

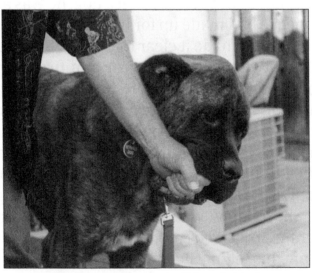

Sharp and Sunny holding hands

Sunny still has special needs, and Sharp is ever faithfully by his side. Sharp is also reported to be very good with children and very patient and gentle with other dogs, even little dogs that for whatever reason seem to think they are able to take him on. The thought of a less than fifteen pound dog of any type trying to take on a 180 pound mastiff boggles the mind. What are they thinking? But Sharp seems to have the patience of Job, and I'm convinced any type of response from him could easily thwart any further threats. Sharp is a gentle giant who is an incredible gatekeeper, always aware of his surroundings and always available to protect not just his owner's physical safety but also his health. As Sunny summed up his interaction with Sharp, "Relationship is everything."

Chapter 19

Sasha

Diamond P Sasha Remeny CGC, TDI

"**E**veryone should have someone in their life that shakes with joy when they come home. I walk through the door and there Sasha is—jumping, carefree, tail wagging. She makes me feel so loved." This was my daughter Erin's reply when I asked her what she appreciates most about her dog, Sasha, a five-year-old, yellow Labrador Retriever. Erin, like all my children, grew up with dogs that she considered four-legged furry friends that you could tell all your secrets to and just love and be loved in return. During trying times in her life Erin found our dogs to be a great source of comfort, and now she has Sasha who never disappoints.

Erin, professionally, is a physical therapy assistant who currently is performing in-home physical therapy. She is experienced working in skilled nursing facilities, is a certified wound therapist, has assisted in spinal cord rehabilitation, traumatic brain injury, burns, outpatient orthopedic care, pediatrics, and sub-acute conditions. It made total sense to me when Erin chose to get a Labrador Retriever. Erin wanted a therapy companion dog, and Labradors have a reputation for being even tempered, well behaved, and are widely accepted and known for their excellence as guide dogs for the blind and their effectiveness as search and rescue dogs. Erin grew up with Dobermans and knew our dogs firsthand, with their excellent temperaments. But amazingly enough, some people seem to be a little resistant to and even shy away from a therapist walking into a therapy session with a Doberman Pinscher . . . can't imagine why . . . just kidding.

Sasha and Erin

Sasha is a well-trained therapy dog, and Erin can use her in many ways. Erin will tell a patient to play with her. To improve the patient's dynamic stabilization for instance, Erin can have Sasha gently pull on a patient (with attached leash) while the patient attempts to hold themselves still. Or Erin can have Sasha stand still while the patient tries to pull her. These will improve the patient's core strength and balance. Another example might be to have the patient pet and stroke Sasha. The dog would hold still while the patient moved forward, backward, and side to side, thus improving the patient's upper extremity range of motion. There are many other possibilities, but I'm thinking that every patient's favorite would probably be stroking the dog's head, gently rubbing her ears, pulling treats apart to give her, all the while maybe not even realizing that those actions are great for improving fine motor control especially for arthritic hands. It is easy to imagine why Sasha might really enjoy her job.

Sasha comes from a wonderful line of working dogs. Her breeder's dogs have been trained for search and rescue, some are hunting champions, as well as others that are accomplished working dogs like Sasha, a licensed therapy dog. They are bred to have the thicker coats so that they can withstand more extreme temperatures when needed. Sasha loves to play in the snow. I can just imagine while the family might be dreaming of hot chocolate inside the cabin, Sasha might prefer to roll around in the snow, chase the wildlife, or explore the surrounding area.

You may now think that Sasha is all work (except for the rolling around in the snow), but no, Sasha loves to play. Sasha was one of nine puppies in her litter, but when Erin went to pick out her puppy there were fourteen puppies to choose from. It might be hard to be together with thirteen other puppies and not get lost in the shuffle, but Sasha, even at a young age, recognized her opportunities for a good prank. This little lady has a sense of humor. As Erin was watching the puppies, Sasha sat on the sidelines and watched her litter sister who had a big pear in her mouth. She was probably thinking how yummy that looked because at just the right optimal moment, Sasha made a mad dash for her sister and snatched that pear and ran for her life with other puppies running behind. This was a foretelling of things to come.

Sasha, an alpha dog, was brought home when she was fourteen weeks old. Erin and her family already had a dog, a lab and chow mix named LB, who, up until Sasha's arrival, had been the alpha dog. But then here comes cute little Sasha girl who would without hesitation pin LB down and try to do some very unladylike things to him. When Sasha was still young, LB would growl at her, but by the time Sasha was an adult, LB gave up trying to get her to change her ways. The alpha role in the home is often exemplified by who gets their choice of bed, who eats first, who goes out first and maintains the lead on walks. I'm sure LB did not appreciate surrendering his place as the alpha dog, but in fairness to Sasha, she also played with him and kept him more active and young especially in his declining years. When I got Kobe, Erin said it was about time that someone put Sasha in her place. She met her match in Kobe. She tried her alpha ways with Kobe and wondered why it wasn't working as well—in fact, not working at all. But Kobe knows how to play nicely and as she gets used to him, he'll keep her young and frolicking just like she did for LB.

One day when I was over visiting, I noticed that Erin had gotten Sasha a "licker license." I asked Erin why, because Sasha is not a licker. "But," Erin replied, "there have been times that have been so difficult for me, and Sasha comes and comforts me and licks my tears away. Sasha is very empathetic, and I don't want to forget what a precious dog I have."

Sasha has a well-balanced life. Her favorite pastimes include tug of war, swimming, and tracking. Aside from her occasional role as a therapy dog, she likes to and needs to work, to do something productive to stay out of mischief. Erin will take her out for a walk, and she will track and find things. Erin doesn't always necessarily want what Sasha finds but is appreciative of her efforts nonetheless. Sasha also loves to be chased and will go out of her way to find a way to make you chase her, and she also loves to chase dogs, people, anything. She's an equal opportunity participant.

Probably the most fun Sasha had was when the family went vacationing in Mendocino. There were nine acres on the beach with lots of wildlife, including raccoons, deer, possums, rabbits, foxes, and skunks. I may have missed a few, but those alone were enough to keep Sasha busy tracking. There were also lots of trails for hiking and climbing that Erin was more than happy to do with her while the rest of the family was otherwise occupied. Sasha seems happiest when she can track and hunt, and up in Mendocino, she was definitely in her element. While they were there, Sasha even got to go on the sightseeing Skunk Train. How many Labradors can claim that fun adventure?

Sasha also has some very unique gifts as a therapy dog. She is very perceptive and tunes in to the needs of humans. She sensed Erin's physical distress as she neared the time of the approaching delivery of her baby. At that time, Sasha was less than a year old. She's always been attached to Erin, but from about twenty-six weeks of Erin's pregnancy, Sasha was always in her lap, at her feet, next to her. There was a definite escalation in Sasha's attentiveness when the time came closer for Paige to be born. In addition to what she was already doing, Sasha would sit at the door and whimper if Erin was behind closed doors. Sasha didn't necessarily want to be touched, but always wanted to maintain visual contact with her. Soft nudges, gentle whimpering, and tireless vigil let Erin know when her time was near.

At that time, Erin didn't fully realize all the signs that Sasha was giving her of her imminent delivery, but Erin was able to apply Sasha's cues to her most recent pregnancy. Not long ago, Erin gave birth to another lovely little girl, Megan Noelle. Megan was due on Christmas Day, but Sasha gave Erin indications that Megan was planning to arrive earlier. Just as before, Sasha again decided that she continually wanted to be in Erin's lap, at her feet, or next to her.

Once when Erin left Sasha at home to pick up Paige from school, Sasha started not only howling, but shaking, whining, scratching nervously, licking her paws, and drooling. Sasha was adamant in not wanting to let Erin out of her sight. And sure enough, Megan arrived early on December 20, and now Sasha has another little girl to love.

Sasha is wonderful with the kids. While she does watch over them, Erin believes that Sasha thinks of herself as one of the kids, not just one that watches them. On their most recent vacation, Sasha watched the kids while they were in the water, ran with them on the beach, and would sun herself next to Josh in the boat. At home, she allows Paige to dress her with a cape, hat, and necklace and models these accessories without complaint. Once Sasha stayed still and allowed Paige to do a chalk outline of her on the back patio. Talk about patience! Of course Sasha knows that Erin will protect her if the kids get carried away or if in some way they are not being good to her. Erin loves Sasha for her gentleness, sweetness, and perceptiveness to the well-being of others, especially children.

Sasha with sleepy Paige

Sasha is not a vocal dog but will make her wishes known. In other words, she wants to do whatever Erin does. On this most recent vacation, Sasha decided she would try to tube with Erin behind the boat. She's not a happy camper when Erin is in the water and she is not with her. So Sasha climbed right into Erin's lap in the inner tube. Fortunately, their inner tube has a mesh net in the center, making the accommodations more comfortable.

Sasha, like most dogs, has her peculiar quirks. She is a nester. She will dig around and around until her bed is just the way she wants it. And whether it's in the creek or in the ocean, Sasha does not walk or run through water but bounds like a deer. Boing! Sasha can be so funny.

I mentioned before that Sasha is not a vocal dog. The first time Erin ever heard Sasha bark, Erin thought there must be an intruder in the house, but in fact, Sasha was stalking Paige's stuffed tiger. Sasha would run up the stairs, run back down the stairs, "woof" at it, and repeat the process. What a clown! What was she thinking? Not that we'll ever know but I prefer to think that she was protecting Paige from the wild animal. The tiger was stuffed, but she didn't figure that out until later. Sasha was a puppy then. Sasha is a good protector and loves her family. She doesn't bark or growl very often, but when she does, there's a reason. Nothing more than that is needed from a faithful gatekeeper.

Chapter 20

Jetta

Jetta the Second, Service Dog #30892

One of the best things about writing this book is that I've had the opportunity to make some new friends and get to know some other friends better. I had the impression that when I met Shelley Smith, the connection was made by divine appointment. Erick and I were leaving church service one Sunday morning, and I noticed Shelley and Jetta in the parking lot. Seeing that Jetta was a service dog, my curiosity was aroused and I immediately thought that this might be a story that needed to be told. Jetta is a three-year-old Yellow Lab and Golden Retriever mix, small for the breeds but that much bigger in heart.

Shelley is the Area Director of Young Life Capernaum ministry. It is a nonprofit organization that ministers to men and women with special needs from teenagers to adults, whom she simply refers to as "friends." The goal of the ministry is to improve their lives through fun, friendship, and adventure while exploring faith in God. The ministry has a small staff of four and a volunteer group of twenty to twenty-five people, including volunteer drivers. Shelley had a vision of the many ways that a service dog would be a blessing and a benefit in her ministry.

The process of acquiring a service dog takes about a year. After an intensive application process, each perspec-

tive handler must attend a two-week program during which time the handlers are given the opportunity to work with a number of different dogs and are closely observed with each one. Then the trainers are also careful to ensure each dog's suitability for what the dog will be used for, as well as observe how well the dog responds to each particular handler. The dog and handler teams are chosen very carefully so that the match is good for both. This process takes absolute determination and perseverance on the part of the new handler.

The dogs begin being prepared to be service dogs from the time they are seven weeks old, although their intensive training begins at seventeen months. Jetta is technically called a facility dog. The difference between a "service dog" and a "facility dog" is that with a facility dog, the owner is not the one who is disabled and needs a companion. The preparation, training, and licensing are identical.

Jetta works with Shelley every day and her sweet, gentle, and loving temperament makes her a wonderful service dog. Shelley says, "Everyone and I mean *everyone* loves her and is thrilled that Jetta is our Young Life dog." Jetta is smart and easily teachable and came to Shelley well prepared for the role she would fulfill. Shelley has had Jetta for about a year now and says that Jetta is "off the charts better and more than she even hoped for."

Jetta is affectionate and very sensitive around the friends with disabilities whom she works with. She seems to know intuitively when to back off if friends are afraid of her or of dogs in general, and she can do service oriented tasks, such as push the "push plate" on a door to get in or out of a building. She's a true companion that can sense what the need is and how she can be of help. Sometimes the best thing she can do is just be there to love and be loved. Even when Jetta is technically working, her job is often fun. She goes on outings with her  group of friends, goes to camp, on ski trips, or just goes on walks or to the park.

Sometimes she gets to just go for coffee because that's one of the things to do in our society. I'm thinking Jetta's too young to drink coffee, but I would bet that if Jetta is loved as much as Shelley says she is, she gets offered as much love and attention as she can handle. Jetta enjoys working one-on-one with her community of friends. They want to help care for her by brushing her, and they learn about the commitment and responsibility that is needed to own an animal. Jetta gives just as much as she gets and often more.

Jetta teaches her friends about unconditional love. I have heard it said many times that we should tell people about the love of God, and only when it's absolutely necessary to use words. People should see God in us by how we treat them. Jetta treats people with gentleness and compassion. Sometimes friends will lie down next to her and just love her and pet her because they know she is safe, and this warm, living, and loving ball of fur will love them in return. And healing takes place.

Recently, Shelley took Jetta to her first camp. There she met three hundred or more typical teenagers as well as the group she went with. Unknown to anyone, one of the teenaged girls suffered from panic attacks. Jetta sensed this and often would work her way over to this girl and by her supportive presence, helped this girl make it through the week. One of the other teenagers, a boy, was going through a rough family situation. He would seek Jetta out and would just hug her and thereby release some of the pain he was feeling. These kids and some of their families who came with them had left dogs at home and would spend time playing with Jetta, making camp feel a little more like home away from home. Jetta is a minister with four legs.

Shelley has expressed her desire for the future to be able to expand her ministry with Jetta by taking Jetta and some of their friends to visit people who are in convalescent care facilities. It would be a way for them to give to others the loving compassion that they themselves have received. I know that when we sow seeds of love into the lives of others, it has a way of bringing a harvest of love back into our own lives.

Jetta lives with Shelley and her husband David, and though I spent only a couple of hours at their home, their love and care for this dog is unquestionable. Shelley says Jetta is such a sweet and sensitive dog to live with. This made the adjustment to living with her natural and easy. There is peace in their home that Jetta thrives on. Occasionally, Shelley and David get excited when they're watching sports on television and have had to learn to be excited without raising their voices because if they do, Jetta will go get in her crate and remain there until the "excitement" is over. (Jetta would not do well at my house when the Golden State Warriors are playing.)

Jetta and Shelley

As much as Jetta enjoys working, she also enjoys her time when her service dog vest comes off. That seems to be her cue that she's now off duty. I wondered what she would do as I watched Shelley remove her vest, and I was delighted to see that she did some of the same things my dog does. To begin with, she sat on my foot and wanted to be petted and gently scratched behind the ears. I could almost hear an "Ahhhhh" coming from her after a good day's work. Shelley and I went out in their backyard, and I watched Shelley play ball with her and found out that like a normal lab, she is ball obsessed.

Jetta also enjoys her walks and apparently also greatly enjoys playing a game with Dave that they call "crazy dog." In this game, Dave will take the dog outside either in the front or backyard and bows down to Jetta saying, "Jetta, crazy dog!" Jetta responds by turning wildly in circular motions and running all over the place. I must admit I feel like doing similar things after a hard day at work. I think this is Jetta's way of "letting her hair down" so to speak, and I bet it feels great!

Jetta also enjoys her walks, though she never breaks her stride to veer away from Shelley as many other dogs would in the course of a nice walk. Jetta doesn't show particular interest in hunting or tracking like most labs, but then she has been prepared to be a service dog from the time she was very young. She still does a lot of fun activities, but she's a lot more serious when she's wearing her vest. In either case, Jetta always looks to Shelley for direction. Shelley says that one of her favorite bonding moments with Jetta is the way she loves to lay her head on Shelley's chest. It's always a very tender moment.

In case you're thinking that Shelley's always in charge, and most of the time she probably is, sometimes, however,

Jetta has her way of getting mom to do what she wants. If she thinks that maybe she's not getting enough attention, Jetta will lie down in Shelley's line of sight with her ball resting right in front of her nose. If Shelley goes somewhere else, Jetta will move to where she can still see mom or more likely where mom can still see her, yep, with the ball in front of her nose. If mom still doesn't get the hint, then Jetta will sometimes go outside and play ball with herself. She's adept at tossing the ball up herself and then getting it. She'll continue to romp around, throw the ball in the pool and jump in and get it. Labs are known to be wonderful swimmers! And when she's refreshed, she'll roll around on the grass with that ball still in her mouth. By this time, Shelley feels duly guilty for not having played with Jetta long enough and will go out to play with her. Just like a loving mother!

And Jetta knows how to be one of the girls. Shelley told me of a time that she took Jetta on a five-day women's retreat (to have some girls' time), and Jetta loved the time away, enjoying fun in the sun and even laying on a raft just enjoying the relaxation.

Jetta is an exceptional gatekeeper only of a slightly different variety. She doesn't normally bark to sound the alarm, although if it's someone she doesn't know who gets too close, she barks. If someone's at the door that she doesn't know, she will stand between Shelley and the visitor until they are either invited in or they leave. Jetta is perimeter trained so she will not cross the threshold without Shelley's direction. When a dog is obviously well trained, it makes people wonder what else she may be trained to do and they will approach with caution if they haven't been invited in. If Jetta's outside playing by herself, she will come inside regularly to check on Shelley and see if she is well. What

Shelley says she most appreciates about Jetta is that she is so steady day after day. Jetta can be trusted and always watches her with eyes of love and acceptance and always looking for direction. The trust works both ways.

Most of us who have dogs love them just because they are who they are and not because of all that they do. But here is a dog with a family who loves her, but Jetta is also a dog with a wonderful purpose. She spends her life enriching the lives of others and for what she is and all that she does, she will be loved and remembered by all the lives she has touched.

Chapter 21

To Serve and Protect

Heroes aren't made in a moment in time when they are in the right place at the right time to do something spectacular that changes lives in some remarkable way. That's only when they are revealed. Heroes are developed by what individuals do and decisions they make day in and day out as part of life and/or part of their duty. Men and women study and train hard to become police officers. That, along with their on-the-job experience, prepares them to make difficult choices during sometimes incredibly stressful situations. Their commitment and daily sacrifice to be ready to help people at a moment's notice is expected of them by the public, and they generally expect it of themselves. Too often these officers as well as their K9 partners, when they are fortunate enough to have them, go unappreciated and are taken for granted. Sometimes they are even opposed and disrespected by the very people they are trying to help. This should not be so.

To become a member of the K9 unit, each officer must apply and indicate why they are interested in a K9 partner. They then must undergo an oral test. During this time they are asked what they've done to prepare themselves to be part of this unit. What basic training have they had? Have they participated as a helper to other officers training their dogs? Have they shown good judgment in handling difficult situations in the field? Is their home such that they have a safe and protected place to keep their dog? Even an officer's proficiency in writing detailed and complete reports is evaluated. Having a canine partner involves the potential for the additional use of force when a serious crime is involved. This of course must be accurately reported and the reasons for the use of the dog substantiated. In addition, an officer must understand that their commitment to the unit would be for a minimum of five years, because their commitment is not only to the department but also to their dogs. I can only conclude that officer candidates applying to be part of the K9 team are proven, seasoned police officers deemed trustworthy to use good judgment when working with these dogs.

Officer Tom Gratney and Argo

Dogs that are deemed good prospects for police work are usually paired with a handler at a year and a half to two years of age and on the average serve until the age of eight or nine years, though sometimes longer depending on the dog's health and well-being. Each dog lives with his officer handler. Even so, these dogs are not considered "pets." These are performance dogs, trained police officers. They are nonetheless a part of the officer's family and interact with the family as a whole within certain guidelines.

Officer Chris Bell and Cezar

The dogs considered for police work are tested for their suitability for this type of work. They must be smart and trainable. These police dogs are intact males and what we would call "alpha dogs"; that is, they are strong, stable, and fearless. They receive basic obedience training before they are chosen for police work, but then they continue their training with their handlers. The bond between the officers and their dogs develop as they train and work together day by day. It often takes about two years of continuous working and living together before the officer and his dog reach a point where they "gel," meaning they have the confidence of knowing what the other will do in any given situation. It is therefore easy to understand the pressure and focus an officer experiences working with his dog to ensure the safety of all involved on a police call.

Recently, I had the privilege of spending a few hours with three of the four members of the Santa Clara Police K9 unit. This unit is headed by Sgt. Kevin Fraser, who previously spent a little more than seven years as part of the team. The current K9 officers present were Officer Nate Crescini and his K9 partner Jax, Officer Chris Bell and his K9 partner Cezar, and Officer Tom Gratney and his K9 partner Argo. Watching these men with their dogs, I developed an understanding of the depth of their commitment to this special unit, to each other, and to their dogs.

Their first and most important purpose and goal is to provide the best possible service to their community while ensuring each other's safety. They work eleven-hour shifts, four days one week and three days the next. Aside from their regular responsibilities responding to calls for help, they spend a minimum of sixteen hours a month doing intensive training with their dogs, to not just maintain their dog's skills but to improve upon them. To maintain their dog's skills, daily maintenance training is expected of each team. In addition to their everyday duties, these K9 units serve as support to other police officers in other cities when their specialized skills are needed.

All of the dogs are well trained in basic obedience. This includes working the dogs around a myriad of distractions such as groups of people, gunfire, scenarios where an arrest is in progress, other dogs, and other weapons officers may have like rubber batons. The intent is to teach the dog to focus on the task at hand and the direction of the officer/

handler. The dogs are taught scent discrimination, tactics for searching for hidden suspects, handler protection, and tracking. Of the current dogs that are part of the team, two are also trained in narcotics detection and two are trained for explosive detection.

Officer Nate Crescini and Jax

Common duties of the K9 units are to secure the perimeter of a building or an area where a search is being conducted. They are also often called to perform the search itself. These dogs have keen senses far superior to people. A K9 unit can complete a search of an area in probably half the time of several police officers alone; first because the dogs are fast and can cover an area far more quickly, but also because they are able to hear the slightest sound, follow a scent, detect and respond to movement, and also sense fear, for example, of a subject in question. Though it was not mentioned at the time of the interview for this story, my personal experience, having had some excellent working dogs, is that these dogs are often also a very good judge of character and can sense when something is amiss. All these qualities make them an invaluable asset not just to the police officer they belong to but to the police department as a whole.

I asked the officers what they considered to be their biggest challenge in working with these dogs in the field. The most mentioned challenge for the officer was remembering that (especially at first) they are working with a two- or three-year-old. Expecting them to be more mature than they are is unrealistic and can become a disappointment and lead to unrealistic expectations. But if they can keep in mind the dog's age and experience, then the partnership is very effective and rewarding in the field.

As I watched these officers train their dogs, I could see that not only do they enjoy working with these dogs but I could also see how deeply the officers care for them. And the feeling is mutual. Being a dog person, I found myself sensitive to the body language of the dogs at least as much as I was watching the training process between dog and handler. Because it was winter time, it was already mostly dark or dark when this training was taking place, even though lighting was provided. Even so, as an example, when it was Nate's turn to work with Jax on basic obedience as well as doing Jax's bite work, this dog focused on Nate, his demeanor demonstrating his unquestionable loyalty and affection. Even in the dark at a distance of approximately seventy-five feet, it was unmistakable that Jax was in tune with Nate's movement, direction, and looked to him with utmost confidence and trust. It was also evident that Jax clearly knows that he is valued and protected. I'm certain this is the case with every one of these dogs and their handlers, as these dogs are treated with the loving respect they are due.

"Unquestionable loyalty and affection"

Chris and Cezar

While officers may send their dogs to apprehend a fleeing suspect, they will not send them into a situation where it is either known or strongly suspected that the suspect has a gun. I asked about the instances of injuries to the dogs in the line of duty. Though most dogs at one time or another get their share of bumps and bruises, all in all, injuries are minimal. There was one cited case within the Santa Clara Police units where a dog had been brutally stabbed multiple times. The dog did survive and served a few more years of duty before being retired. I was very much impressed and relieved to know that this department has never lost a dog in the line of duty.

Ricky

As a side note, I think it's a natural thing (at least I hope it is) that even in pursuing a story as important as this one, I found myself tempted to ask some off-the-wall questions. Fortunately for me, these officers are genuinely nice people who didn't mind answering an occasional "unusual" question. One pressing question on my mind at the time was, "I've observed that police dogs always ride in the back of the police vehicle. If you, as a K9 unit, are called out to a crime in progress, apprehend the suspect who is then arrested and needs to be transported to the police station, does the dog then get to ride up front?" The obvious answer, which in hindsight I realize should have occurred to me, was that another unit is called to transport the prisoner. But in the cold night as I was watching these dogs work, I had visions of the prisoner on his or her absolutely best behavior under the watchful eye of the canine officer. I couldn't help but smile.

Excellent care of their dog is primary to each K9 officer. This includes regular veterinary care, quality food provided, and regular water and bathroom breaks during the workday so the dog remains comfortable and at his best. Whether or not the officer is in the car, the motor is left running with the temperature carefully controlled for the safety and well-being of the dog. Should the conditions in the car change while the officer is out of the vehicle (such as a failure of the air conditioner), an alert is immediately transmitted to the officer so that he can intervene.

As well as these dogs are treated by the officers, it is not always the case with the public. I was stunned to learn that prior to July of 1984, it was not a criminal offense to injure a police dog. Since that time, it is illegal (not to mention unjust and to me, unthinkable) to poison, shoot, stab, or injure a dog in any manner while he is under the supervision of a police officer. Our municipal code takes that law a step further indicating that it is a crime to willfully interfere with a police dog in the performance of his duty under the direction of his police officer/handler. I cannot even imagine the logic behind why anyone would intentionally injure or even antagonize or harass a trained police dog. Talk about enticing the dog to want to take a "bite out of crime." I am glad to know that these dogs are now legally protected and any of the above-mentioned offenses are citable.

Like any human officer, the dogs need their down time to relax and renew their energy. When the dogs are released by their handler, whether it's by command, removing of their working collar, or simply just by virtue of being home, they know that their workday is over. The dogs also need to have fun. While they are considered police officers, they are also still dogs that love to play ball, go for walks, dig holes in the sand at the beach, and the other normal things that most dogs look forward to. I'm thinking that since they're alpha dogs, like my Kobe, their favorite game is probably tug-of-war.

Nate and Jax playing a game of tug of war

As I briefly mentioned before, these dogs live with their officer partners and their families. These dogs are well socialized, able to relatively easily adapt to family life, which generally includes children, and even other dogs that are pets, without issue. Though the dog's primary bond is with the officer, they have loving relationships with the other family members.

Sergeant Kevin Fraser and Ricky

Sgt. Kevin Fraser shared with me an example of just how much these dogs become family, and it deeply touched my heart. One of Kevin's partners while he served with the K9 unit was a German Shepherd named Ricky. Ricky became his partner when Kevin and his wife were expecting their daughter Alex. Alex grew up with Ricky and it was very difficult for her as well as for the rest of the family when Ricky passed. The following is a letter from a young girl's heart to her lifelong friend.

Alex and Ricky

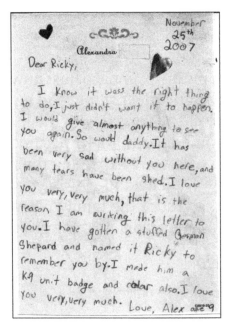

November 25th 2007

Alexandra

Dear Ricky,

I know it wass the right thing to do, I just didn't want it to happen. I would give almost anything to see you again. So would daddy. It has been very sad without you here, and many tears have been shed. I love you very, very much, that is the reason I am writing this letter to you. I have gotten a stuffed German Shepard and named it Ricky to remember you by. I made him a K9 unit badge and color also. I love you very, very much. Love, Alex age 9

P.S. It was sad to see you go because you have been there for me all my life, all 9 years.

These pictures that Alex drew of Ricky were times when she dressed him up in her costume jewelry and other things that she thought looked good on him. He was obviously very tolerant of the antics of a little girl who dearly loved him and the time she spent with him. Ricky is a great example of a loving, solid tempered working dog with great character and great patience.

Since I was motivated to write this story, I asked the officers a question they didn't seem to expect: "If there was one thing you'd want people to know about you (as an officer), what would it be?" The bottom line answer I received was this: "We are here to help people. If you're driving and you see a police car with the lights flashing, with or without a siren, pull over! Failure to do so impedes the police officer's ability to do his job. Sometimes, those few wasted minutes could result in the loss of someone's life." These police officers go out of their way to make themselves available for our community to be able to get to know them. They do demonstrations with their dogs at the police station, at schools, churches, and other venues made available to them. It is their desire for there to be understanding and cooperation between them and the people they serve.

"To serve and protect" is not only a logo that is sometimes written on the sides of police vehicles. It is what police officers do every day. They do what they can to enable us to live in peace and safety. An appropriate response to what they do, because of all that they do, is to honor them with the courtesy and respect they deserve, along with their K9 partners, as the gatekeepers of our community.

Santa Clara Police Department K9 Unit

"K9 Police, the next generation"

Final Thoughts

Thank you for sharing my love and appreciation for dogs through *Tails of the Gatekeepers*. I hope you have enjoyed reading these stories as much as I have loved sharing them. Each one was special to me in some way. Those dogs that are no longer with us will always be remembered, and those that are with us will continue to fill our lives with fun, joy, and adventures.

I would not have traded any of the time I've had with the dogs (and occasionally a cat) in our family. My children grew up learning to enjoy dogs while learning to treat animals with kindness and respect. I also would not have missed meeting and knowing a lot of wonderful people and their dogs, many of whom I consider good and lasting friends.

I trust that many of you have learned about some less well-known dogs and have enjoyed the process. When I started working Kobe, many people asked me how I got him in such great condition. And as I mentioned in Kayla's story, I would tell people, "Kobe runs with a Vizsla!" More times than not, their response would be, "What's a Vizsla?" Therein is my desire to introduce Vizslas to people beyond the show ring. It was a similar story with the Rhodesian

Ridgebacks, as well as with a few other breeds. I probably learned the most and feel enriched for the experience.

I've already been encouraged to write a sequel to *Tails of the Gatekeepers*. When I find dogs whose stories should be shared, the sequel will follow.

My thanks to you all!
Elizabeth C. Chapman

CPSIA information can be obtained at www.ICGtesting.com
Printed in the USA
BVOW10s1448130514

353323BV00002B/2/P